Claudia w ...
school yea ...
up a class together. But now Anna was ill and Claudia would
have to start the new term on her own.

In Anna's absence, Claudia befriends the new girl, Sylvie,
and on Anna's return the twosome inevitably becomes a
threesome. The three all go off to stay by the sea with
Claudia's great-aunt Belle - but Claudia finds it difficult to
share her aunt with the others and is jealous of the attention
Belle gives them, particularly Anna.

Belle is fully aware that Claudia feels that she doesn't fit in
anywhere - be it with her schoolfriends or at home with her
mother and Wilf Smee - and it is partly through Belle that
Claudia comes to understand that she does fit in and that she
does belong.

Another book by Gina Wilson
CORA RAVENWING

Gina Wilson

ALL ENDS UP

PUFFIN BOOKS
in association with
Faber and Faber

Puffin Books, Penguin Books Ltd, Harmondsworth, Middlesex, England
Viking Penguin Inc., 40 West 23rd Street, New York, New York 10010, U.S.A.
Penguin Books Australia Ltd, Ringwood, Victoria, Australia
Penguin Books Canada Limited, 2801 John Street, Markham, Ontario, Canada L3R 1B4
Penguin Books (N.Z.) Ltd, 182–190 Wairau Road, Auckland 10, New Zealand

First published by Faber and Faber Limited 1984
Published in Puffin Books 1986

Typeset, printed and bound in Great Britain by
Hazell Watson & Viney Ltd,
Member of the BPCC Group
Aylesbury, Bucks
Filmset in VIP Plantin

For Elizabeth Burdon

1

People had been saying for years that Candlemaker Row should be pulled down. They said it was the shame of Ratfield – a pig shouldn't be asked to live there. Claudia Spark and her mother occupied Number Nine. On either side, the houses were boarded up, awaiting repair before new Council tenants could be installed. But Claudia's mother actually owned Number Nine. Her aunt had bought it for her from the Council, in the days before the rot set in. The street had been pretty then, with window boxes and cobbles. Claudia had been brought here as an infant, direct from Ratfield Maternity Hospital. Aunt Belle had been waiting on the doorstep as Fern Spark clambered from the taxi with her bundle.

Now Claudia was fourteen and a pupil of the sprawling Comprehensive school on the outskirts of the town. Her teachers found her resilient and resourceful – the sort who made a good job of being monitor, did homework at the right time and could be relied upon to get sixty plus in any examination. The only person who spoke at all disparagingly of her was the mother of Anna Hackman, her best friend. But nobody suited Mrs Hackman.

Claudia was standing at her bedroom window. She had just been speaking to Anna on the phone. In the background, Mrs Hackman had been yapping away, so Anna's message had been brief. She was ill again. She wouldn't be at school the next day – probably not for a fortnight. Claudia leaned her head against the pane. Tomorrow was the first day of the new school year. She and Anna were moving up into Mr Carpenter's class. Everything would be upside down for a day or two till people got the hang of it. But now Anna wasn't going to be there at all.

Idly, she watched the tramps congregating at the wooden bench opposite. Anna always said they made her feel sick, and how could Claudia bear living on top of them. That was Mrs Hackman talking, of course. All the same, it wasn't particularly nice knowing such thoughts were lingering in your friend's head every time you asked her round especially as, on the inside, Number Nine was very spruce. Fern had covered the floors with Chinese matting and made curtains from Laura Ashley prints. She'd stripped old chests and wardrobes to the bare wood and polished them. In the tiny living-room were wicker armchairs and a sofa with spotted cushions. Aunt Belle had bought a pine table and stools for the kitchen, where Fern kept a vase of fresh flowers on the window-sill all the year round. Upstairs were two immaculate small bedrooms and a bathroom with a pale yellow suite. In the midst of squalor, Number Nine was a showpiece.

Without any conscious feelings of pleasure or relief, Claudia caught sight of her mother. She was picking her way over the cobbles with her coat and hair flapping in the wind and a plastic shopping bag banging against her legs. Why did Fern always look flustered? Why couldn't she even button her coat? Claudia turned away from the window. She didn't want to hear if the winos called after her mother. She didn't want to catch their remarks. She was coming down the stairs as Fern pushed open the front door, filling the hall with the smell of vinegar and hot newspaper. 'I've got us fish and chips. Get some plates out.'

In Winchester Road, Dr Sylvester was backing out of the front door of the Hackmans' three-bedroomed semi. Mrs Hackman was thanking him for coming. 'I wouldn't have bothered you, Doctor, except that I knew you could pop in on your way home from surgery. It's not really out of your way, is it? I'd hate to put you out.'

Dr Sylvester's hand was on his car door-handle. 'She'll live, Mrs Hackman. You mustn't panic. Bring her down to the surgery next week if she's no better.'

Mrs Hackman watched as the silver Volvo slid away from the kerb. She closed the front door and crept back across the linoleum towards the stairs. Her husband, Frank, was marking in the front room. He marked every evening between six and nine-thirty, that being the only way to keep his head above water, he said. She'd reached the foot of the stairs before he called out. He was sitting with a pile of exercise books on his knees and another at his feet. 'What did the doctor say?'

'He thought I was making a fuss. You know what they're like these days. Unless you're at death's door, it's all aspirins and glasses of water.'

'Do you think you could settle yourself in one spot for the next hour or so? I can't concentrate when you're trailing about like a lost soul.'

Cynthia Hackman withdrew meekly, shutting out the sight of Frank's pudgy pale face with its toothbrush moustache, and his knees drawn up to his chest. He'd relax later. There was a letter from their son, Ralph. She'd kept it for a surprise.

These days, the Hackmans were doing something uncharacteristic and, given their temperaments, foolish. They had begun to live beyond their means. Two years ago they had sent Ralph away to a major public school. They had hoped he would win a scholarship but, when he hadn't, they'd sent him just the same. There had been a small legacy from an uncle to draw on at first and some Post Office savings. But now they were trying to foot the bills out of Frank's salary as science master at a local boys' school, and it was beginning to look as if it couldn't be done.

'Is Dad marking?' whispered Anna as Mrs Hackman slipped into her room.

'Don't talk,' said Mrs Hackman. 'You've strained your throat already, chatting on to Claudia.'

'What did the doctor say?'

'A virus. I'm going to keep you at home for at least a fortnight. I'm going to get you really fit this time. I really would have thought the week by the sea would have done the trick.' Mrs Hackman perched on the edge of Anna's bed and sighed. 'I'm so vexed when I think of all the work you'll miss. I'll pop into school and collect some homework. At least it's a chance to get ahead with your music – there's always that.'

'I might as well be at school if you're planning a whole lot of homework.'

Mrs Hackman turned sharply. 'If it wasn't for all my effort you wouldn't be half as well on as you are, my girl. Not that I grudge you that. If Dad and I are going to spend all our money on Ralph's education, the least we can do is expend our energies on yours.'

'But I'm supposed to be ill.'

'You like being top in everything, don't you? That doesn't happen without hard work. Sometimes I feel exhausted too, you know.'

Anna sat up anxiously. 'I know, Mum. I'd be useless without you.'

Mrs Hackman managed a smile. She patted Anna's pillow. 'You've got a quick little brain. Give it a good rest and it'll be all ready to leap into action first thing.' She went away, leaving a low light burning in the corner of the room. Anna couldn't sleep without it. If they turned it off late at night she woke, screaming.

Anna listened to the stairs creaking under her mother as she tiptoed downstairs. In the front room, her father's moustache would be twitching and his heels tapping. Everybody in this house was a nervous wreck. She lay back, aching all over. Her blankets had slipped to one side but the effort required to drag them back again was beyond her. An enormous weight seemed to have been lowered over her entire body, pressing it steadily down into the mattress . . .

She and Claudia had been looking forward to tomorrow. They'd talked about it all the time at Aunt Belle's. It would be completely different in Mr Carpenter's class. You had lockers instead of desks and went to all sorts of different classrooms for lessons instead of staying put. Now, everybody would be getting into the swing of it except her. Claudia might even pal up with someone else. It was hard to think who, though. Everyone would know Anna was coming back. They wouldn't want to mess up existing friendships just for the sake of a week or two. More likely Claudia would have to tag on where she could. She'd sounded very fed up on the phone.

Anna could picture her in the poky hall in Candlemaker Row. Poor Cloddie, having to make a go of it in that grotty street with no father and Fern Spark for a mother. Fern was vague and arty and out all the time. Once Anna had heard her own mother snapping that Fern Spark was irresponsible and a drain on society. Mrs Hackman had choked to a halt, seeing Anna in the doorway. It was iniquitous, she'd muttered, how they were paupered by taxes to keep ne'er-do-wells in luxury. Anna hadn't been sure whether Fern Spark was included amongst the 'ne'er-do-wells' but she'd suspected that she was – which had made it all the more surprising when, ten days ago, her parents had raised no objection to the suggestion that she accompany Claudia on one of her regular visits to Fern's aunt. The point was, of course, that, in their present financial straits, the Hackmans could hardly turn down the offer of a free seaside holiday, but, even so, Anna had been astonished to find herself dispatched on the bus to Tod Pool. She had been ill all summer with glandular fever. Aunt Belle had taken one look at her and announced she was going to put half a stone on that skeleton by the end of the week. And she nearly had.

The week had been utterly unlike any other Anna had ever spent. She had never met anyone like Aunt Belle or stayed in a house as big as Tod Pool. She and Claudia had shared a room far away from Aunt Belle's, and Aunt Belle had said she couldn't care less when they went to sleep or when they woke up. They were old enough to make that sort of decision for themselves and she wasn't interested in them if they couldn't. During the day, Aunt Belle inhabited the kitchen and the sitting-room. If they wanted her, she said, that was where she'd be. Otherwise, the run of the house was theirs. After big breakfasts at ten o'clock they took apples from a mottled blue bowl in the middle of the scrubbed kitchen table and vanished till four or five. When they came back, there was soup and stew and baked potatoes for supper. Aunt Belle stoked up the Aga and let them put their feet on the rail along the front while she poured mugs of cider from an earthenware jug. An acquaintance with alcohol was best made in the home, she said . . . There were lots of things about the week that Anna hadn't seen fit to tell her parents. She had come home glowing and plump and they had been pleased. – And now she was back where she'd started.

In the middle of the night, Anna called out in her sleep. Mrs Hackman felt her head and, by the light of the night-lamp, poured water into a glass and dissolved two aspirins. 'I keep thinking about Cloddie,' Anne murmured. 'It'll be awful for her tomorrow all on her own. She'll have no one to go around with.'

Mrs Hackman rattled a teaspoon in the glass. 'I'm sure you don't need to worry about Claudia. She can take care of herself.'

Claudia was sitting in the back row. This was great. You could just wander along to the right classroom and pick any seat. Miss Lever was spreading a complicated calculation over the blackboard. Periodically she stepped aside so that everyone could see, then she leaned forward, removed one or two numbers with the corner of her duster, and replaced them with others, remarking that her reasons for doing so should be obvious. Claudia copied the whole thing down in her rough book and hoped that it would make sense later. Outside, the gardener was mowing the playing-field, rumbling up and down on his motor-mower, sweeping round in a wide arc at the end of each row . . . 'Claudia, I think I might ask you to explain this whole process to the class in a moment or two,' Miss Lever was saying. 'Will you feel equal to that?' The boys laughed loudly and the new girl smiled sympathetically as Claudia's face went red.

The new girl's name was Sylvie Lamont. It had been nice to have her to talk to at morning break. Mr Carpenter had introduced them specially and given them permission to stay inside if they wanted so that Claudia could show Sylvie round the school.

Maths was the last lesson before dinner. Miss Lever chose not to make an example of Claudia but kept her behind instead to say that she'd had good reports of her last year's work and hoped similar standards would be maintained. 'Otherwise,' she said, scooping a pile of books under one arm, 'you won't last long in this set.'

Claudia was left smarting in the empty classrooom.

'What did she say?' whispered Sylvie Lamont, looking in round the door.

Claudia glared at her. 'Piss off!'

In the canteen, Claudia saw Sylvie again. She had taken a place at one of the hot-dinner tables and was beginning to unpack her sandwiches. 'You can't sit there,' bawled Clive Finnegan, sliding his plate of spaghetti the length of the table. 'This is for hot dinners, *idiot*!'

Clive Finnegan was a pig. Anyone deserved to be rescued from him. 'Sit here,' Claudia shouted, and Sylvie, clutching her sandwiches to her chest, scurried towards her. 'Sorry about before,' said Claudia. 'It was Lever picking on me.' During the next ten minutes, others joined their table, as many as half a dozen, but made no attempt to join in their conversation. Claudia Spark was making an effort to be nice to the new girl. No one else need bother.

Sylvie, like Claudia, was just fourteen, only two days separated their birthdays. They were among the oldest in the class – unlike Anna, who was far and away the youngest. By rights, Anna should have been in the class below but Mrs Hackman wouldn't hear of it – Anna came top in every examination and always had. This would have been insufferable but for the fact that it was common knowledge she was pushed to death at home. 'Everyone says she'll be useless at ever thinking for herself,' Claudia told Sylvie. 'She's only OK as long as her parents clue her up on the right answers. She's nice, though. It's awful she's ill all the time. She's my best mate.'

Sylvie nodded. Her parents weren't too bothered about her school work, she said. They'd exhausted themselves worrying about her twin brothers.

'Mum minds about me,' Claudia said. 'She wants me to get a decent job.'

Sylvie looked surprised. 'My parents just assume we'll all go to university. Dad's a lecturer, you see, and Mum's got a degree.'

'My mum's doing an Open University course,' said Claudia, pulling open her crisps and crunching noisily. 'She says you can't get a good job without qualifications. We need the money, you see.'

'I think we're OK for money,' said Sylvie.

'I haven't got a father,' said Claudia. 'I've never had one. My mum's not married.'

*

When Fern Spark came into the kitchen that evening, Claudia was at the sink, stabbing the eyes out of potatoes. She didn't turn round.

'What kind of a first day?' asked Fern.

'Stinking first day, since you ask.' Claudia dropped the peeler into the sink with a spalsh and began dredging the water with her fingers for the bits. 'Anna wasn't there, which I knew. And instead I was plagued by a new girl whose father's a lecturer or something, in London.'

'Who cares what her father does? You can shake her off if she's putting you down.'

'She's not putting me down.' Claudia lit the gas under the potatoes and took sausages from the fridge.

'I've brought us some fish,' said Fern. 'Sit down and I'll see to it.'

She slipped an arm round Claudia as if to steer her towards a stool, but Claudia shrugged savagely. 'It's all your bloody fault,' she hissed.

It wasn't so bad once the meal was on the table and they were sitting in the lamp-light with the orange enamel teapot that Belle had given them. Fern leaned forward on her elbows. 'Still wishing you'd been adopted?' she whispered.

Claudia shook her head. 'Not at this precise moment.'

'Tell me about Sylvie.'

'She's OK. But they've got pots of money, so I don't want her coming here. It's bad enough having to say I haven't got a dad.'

Fern sighed. 'You don't have to say that straight off. Loads of people haven't. There're all sorts of reasons for not having one. You don't have to spell it out as soon as you meet anyone.'

'Might as well. Gets it over with. It always comes out in the end.'

'It's so old-fashioned to think people mind.'

'*I* mind.'

Fern shoved her stool back from the table. 'I'll have to turn the telly on. – Adults don't care, you know. It's just your silly lot. I suppose it's your age. I suppose you stand around sniggering about sex all the time.'

'Well, at least we're not *doing* it.'

'*Bitch!*' Fern snatched her coat from the back of the door and dashed down the passage to the front door.

'I thought it was your University programme,' shouted Claudia, but the front door was banging and Fern was running off along Candlemaker Row.

Sylvie Lamont waited for Claudia by the coat-pegs next morning. 'You can come home for tea after school, if you like. I told Mum your mother was usually out till about six.'

A thought of Anna stirred at the back of Claudia's mind. She would take a dim view of Claudia off out to tea with new friends while she was suffering.

'Will you come?' said Sylvie. 'I'm dying to have someone round.'

Claudia nodded. It wasn't as if Sylvie particularly wanted *her*. Anyone would have done.

East Edge was a couple of miles from the town centre. Claudia and Sylvie managed the journey on Sylvie's bicycle, Sylvie standing on the pedals and Claudia perched behind on the saddle. At first, they wobbled nervously along in the gutter of the main road as lorries roared past with only inches to spare, but the last part of the journey was down a narrow leafy lane. 'Listen to the birds,' said Sylvie over her shoulder, but Claudia could only hear the wind and the whirr of the bicycle wheels.

The house was red brick – bulky and inelegant. 'It's vast,' muttered Claudia, sliding off the saddle. 'You could fit twenty of ours in this. It's as big as my aunt's house.'

'The whole point of leaving London was to have somewhere big and countrified. Dad's got to commute now, you see. We had to get something really nice to make it worthwhile.'

They walked round the house, looking in at windows. Some were curtained but others were bare, as were the rooms beyond. 'We've only been here about a month,' said Sylvie. In one of the rooms a pale-haired woman was holding a picture against the wall and squinting at it from arm's length. 'Mum! She can't decide where to put any of the pictures.' Sylvie rapped the window and the woman jumped and clutched her chest. 'She's terrified! She thinks we're going to be burgled and she's going to have her throat slit!' Sylvie's mother was faded, Claudia thought, as Mrs Lamont struggled with the window-catch. Her hair had been fair, her eyes blue and presumably her cheeks pink but now everything looked washed-out. She was years older than Fern. She had a nice smile, though, when Sylvie introduced them. A devoted maternal type, Claudia decided. Living for her family.

A wide pebble pathway circled the house and, beyond that, flower-beds set in patchy turf bounded by a yew hedge. Sylvie led the way through an archway in the hedge. 'It's the next bit I really like,' she said. 'It's all wild and jungly. Dad says we're going to leave it that way. Jack and Ray have got air guns. They're going to shoot rabbits and pigeons for us to eat.' Claudia pulled a face. 'You don't have to worry. They won't hit anything.'

Over tea, Claudia decided that that was the best thing about Sylvie – and, she suspected, studying Mrs Lamont's tired face, her mother too – she wasn't looking for things to raise her hackles about. She wasn't spoiling for a fight. The trouble with Anna was that she had fixed views on everything – usually her parents' views. 'Principles', she called them. You couldn't disagree with Anna.

At five o'clock the twin brothers returned on bikes from Ratfield Boys' School. 'Mum and Dad didn't want us all at the same school,' Sylvie explained. 'They thought I'd just be written off as the Lamonts' kid sister. I've always been at a different school.'

The twins cut themselves slices of bread from the loaf on the table and spread them with peanut butter. They didn't sit down. 'Were you still scared today, Mum?' said Raymond. His hair was wavy and thick, like Sylvie's, but his face was a mass of red spots and his voice was too loud. Jack blocked his ears and pulled a face at Claudia. He was blond and smooth-skinned and altogether easier to look at than his brother.

In the end, it was handsome Jack who took Claudia home, as Mrs Lamont considered it safer for her to balance on his crossbar than on Sylvie's saddle. He set off with a jerk, throwing her back

16

against his chest and she cowered there, clutching a handful of his sweater, all the way into town. At traffic lights near Candlemaker Row she slipped off and hopped on to the pavement. 'Mum mustn't see. She'd have a fit. I can easily make it from here.' Then she turned and ran off up the street.

2

noting are about that she cannot carry on about a backbiter his more spiteful as well as at it; it truly, it always claims for quarrel. No would not around suppose with to the downstairs with the trouble gases said if given table I am candidly now. If leant they I am running right now go amidly have.

Anna Hackman heard of Sylvie Lamont's existence from Claudia, on the telephone. It was unwelcome news. It was bad enough to be stuck at home, undergoing one of her mother's crash programmes for all-round improvement, without having her best friend choose this moment to desert her. She sat in her bedroom at her small desk and watched the clock tick round to ten-thirty. For the next twenty minutes she did nothing. Claudia and Sylvia would be buying biscuits in the canteen and strolling round the playing field arm in arm. She felt a flood of relief when she knew break time was over. Now they'd be in much the same position as herself, stuck with work they didn't want to do and unable to talk. Her anguish returned at lunch time – the best part of the school day, when she and Claudia shared a table with half a dozen others. Sylvie would be in *her* seat now. When she went back there wouldn't be a space. At home, Anna picked at her food.

'I know perfectly well what's the matter with you,' said Mrs Hackman. 'You think Claudia and the new girl will leave you out when you go back.'

'It'll be awful. Everyone else will've got the hang of the new system. What if Claudia just ignores me?'

Mrs Hackman scraped Anna's leavings into a plastic pedal bin. 'I haven't a scrap of sympathy for you, you know. Firstly, Claudia has never been my idea of an ideal companion. Secondly, if she abandons you at this point, it'll simply prove she's not much of a friend at all, so she'll be no great loss. Thirdly, I wish to goodness you'd look on the bright side. You could make friends with Sylvie yourself. I must say they sound a rather nice family – educated people with a great big house. That would beat visits to Candlemaker Row, wouldn't it? You'll have to grow up a bit, Anna. Being bosom buddies with Claudia Spark will get you nowhere. I've never been happy about you going to her house. It's extremely unhealthy down there. Not what any mother would want for her daughter. I'm quite sure it's not what Fern Spark wants for Claudia.' She started to run water into a bowl in the sink, whisking the suds with her dish-mop and adding under her breath, 'She's got herself to thank for that, of course.'

'Threesomes are no good,' moaned Anna. 'Everyone knows that.'

Mrs Hackman was scrubbing at pans. She talked fast. 'You'll have to stop whining and pull yourself together. Anyway, if you don't start eating square meals soon, heaven knows when you'll get back to school – I'm not sending you while you're pecking like a sparrow.' She turned suddenly to scrutinize Anna, then rushed towards her with dripping hands. 'Oh, don't look so tragic, darling! It'll all turn out all right. It always does. You'll see.' She hugged Anna tight, then held her away and stared again. Her face was quivering. 'Don't drive me mad with your woes, Anna. You're draining my life away.'

Upstairs again, Anna applied herself earnestly to the maths that had been set for the day and later Mrs Hackman came up to mark it. Anna closed her eyes, waiting for the deep sighs that would mean there were mistakes. Mrs Hackman agonized over every error. 'What are we going to do if you can't make a go of it in the State system? What on earth will we do?' Usually Anna didn't reply on these occasions. There was no point in protesting that she *was* making a go of it. Mrs Hackman, looking down at her scattering of red crosses, would simply retort that, if that was so, standards at the Comprehensive must be so abysmal that making a go of it there meant nothing in any case.

Today, however, everything was correct. The pages were a mass of ticks and Mrs Hackman was beaming. 'Clever girl!' she said warmly. They went downstairs to the dining-room where Mrs Hackman kept her piano, a heavy German upright purchased years ago at an auction and promised to Anna in the fullness of time. 'Ralph's education is bleeding us dry,' Mrs Hackman would whisper in her ear. 'We're all suffering. But I'm going to make it up to you, Anna. You'll have all my things. Everything's coming to you. Ralph's having his share now. Yours is to come. It'll all be fair in the end – when we're gone. You'll see.'

Anna sat down at the stool and began to open her music while Mrs Hackman pulled up a chair beside her and closed her eyes. 'Start with the Beethoven,' she said. 'Concert Time. I'm going to sit back and enjoy it.'

'Oh, not Concert Time yet,' protested Anna. 'I'm not up to that. I've only been doing it a fortnight.'

'*Concert Time*,' repeated Mrs Hackman, squeezing her eyes shut.

Anna started to play. 'Please God, let me get through it,' she prayed.

Concert Time was when Anna was expected to produce a performance of a piece rather than a run-through for practice. It was supposed to be the climax of all the work Mrs Hackman had put in with her. It had to be perfect. On top of the piano lay a single Chinese chopstick. Visitors always inspected it curiously, and asked Anna what it was doing there. She never told them. The chopstick was a relic of her earliest days at the keyboard. When she'd been six or seven, after a less than satisfactory Concert Time, her mother had been in the habit of reaching for it and cracking it across her knuckles. The chopstick wasn't used now. There was generally no need for it. In any case, a day had come when Anna was about ten, when she had turned such a strange blank stare on her mother, after being struck, that Mrs Hackman had found herself mumbling apologies. She hadn't used the stick again. It just stayed there, on top of the piano, as a warning to both of them.

Anna brought the piece to a close with two staccato chords and Mrs Hackman opened her eyes. 'Brilliant!' she breathed. 'When you play like that I know it's all worth it.' She opened a book of short pieces by Khatchaturian and, for the next hour, they puzzled over notes and rhythms before Mrs Hackman remembered the time and hurried out for shopping. It was half past five. Anna watched from the front-room window till her mother was out of sight, then she raced to the telephone. There was a minute or two before Mr Hackman came in. 'Don't let her be at Sylvie's,' she muttered, dialling Claudia's number.

*

'Anna's having a really terrible time. Her mother makes her do school work all day. It's amazing. Much harder than the stuff we do at school. That's why she's always top. She's miles ahead of everyone, really.'

Claudia and Sylvie were at East Edge. Claudia had been going nearly every day. She had been taking her bike to school so that she could cycle out to Sylvie's if she was invited, and make her own way home again. To avoid any indebtedness to the Lamonts, she had promised Fern not to eat anything while she was there, so she generally left when Jack and Raymond came in from school. Raymond usually tried to persuade her to stay. 'You don't need to clear off just because we've come home.'

'She's scared of us,' Jack would say. 'Can't you tell?'

'Poor Anna,' said Sylvie now. 'What's the point of it? I thought you said she was too young for our class anyway.'

'The point of it,' said Claudia, 'is to make her as good as her brother who's at boarding school. Mr and Mrs Hackman are ravaged with guilt, Mum says, because they're spending a fortune on Ralph and nothing on Anna.'

'My parents make a big point of treating us all exactly the same. They're against private schools anyway. They think they're anti-social.'

'Ralph Hackman's supposed to be a genius. Mr and Mrs Hackman think they've got to kill themselves to give him the best.'

'Best!' scoffed Sylvie. 'Those places are full of creeps who haven't a clue about anyone else.'

Claudia shrugged. 'The Hackmans must think differently. Actually, they're all nerve cases. Mr Hackman teaches at St Anthony's and stays late to do extra coaching. When he comes home the house has to be silent as a morgue so he can get on with his marking. Then he gulps down a sardine sandwich or something and starts working again. He writes clever-clever textbooks. Mrs Hackman's had a nervous breakdown.'

'Is Anna twitchy too?'

'Not really. You'll see for yourself soon. She's coming back on Monday.'

Sylvie twiddled the fringes of her bedspread. She'd brought

21

Claudia upstairs to her bedroom where she kept her own tape-recorder and tapes. 'D'you think she'll like me? D'you think we could stick together as a threesome? I know she's your best mate really but it's been nice this fortnight, hasn't it?'

'It'll be OK,' said Claudia. 'When she's got used to the idea.'

As she cycled home, Claudia had to admit to herself that it might not be that easy. Anna had been sounding increasingly pinched and mean-minded on the 'phone. 'You haven't completely forgotten me, have you?' she'd said the day before. 'I trust you're remembering what I'm going through, stuck in this miserable hole, swotting my eyes out. I hope you've made quite sure that Sylvie knows all about me.'

'Course I have. I had to talk to someone, didn't I? Or did you think I should give up all human company till you managed to get yourself in one piece again? She's nice. She actually wants to be friends with you too.'

Anna had adopted a wheedling tone. 'Oh, Cloddie, we're all right as we are. We don't need anyone else. I can see just what you're at, you know. You're thinking you'll have the two of us eating out of your hand. After all the years we've been friends . . .'

Claudia and Anna had known each other for eight years. They took a pride in telling people so and rehearsing the story of how they'd first become friends at Hillgrove Primary, in Miss Strang's class, when Anna had been wrongly accused of making a puddle in a corner and Claudia had stuck up for her. '. . . Now someone else turns up while I'm away for a few days and you forget all about me.'

'Shut up,' Claudia had snapped. 'I haven't forgotten about you. You haven't given me the chance. Every time the phone rings, my heart sinks in case it's you, slipping in a quick call while your mum and dad are out. And I know you're just going to nag.'

In the end, they had both apologized and agreed that it had been a miserable fortnight. But now it was almost over. Next week Anna would turn up in Mr Carpenter's class and things would start getting back to normal.

At first, on Monday morning, everything went unbelievably smoothly. When Claudia walked into the classroom at ten to nine,

Sylvie and Anna were already talking, lounging against a radiator together like old pals. As Claudia approached, it was Sylvie who acknowledged her first. Anna's greeting was perfunctory. She didn't actually meet Claudia's eye at all. Claudia smiled to herself. Anna was demonstrating her independence. It was a good sign. The trouble was that Anna continued in this way all day. At lunch time, someone else was absent, so there was no problem about seats. Anna settled Sylvie between herself and Claudia, and then plied her with non-stop questions so that her head was constantly turned away from Claudia. At the end of the afternoon, Sylvie asked them both home. 'Oh, I wish I could come,' Anna said. 'But I'm only allowed out at weekends. You'll have to make do with Cloddie.'

Claudia found herself refusing also. Sylvie obviously didn't care whom she asked as long as she had someone. Serve her right to end up with no one for a change. 'I can't come either,' she said. 'Mum wants me home.'

Sylvie eyed Claudia's bike in surprise. 'I thought you only brought your bike to get back from our house.'

Claudia pedalled away disconsolately. She might have expected this to happen. It was typical of how threesomes operated. There would now be an unending succession of different combinations of twosome plus one hanger-on. Today Sylvie and Anna had been all over each other. Tomorrow it might be herself and Sylvie and the next day herself and Anna. Nobody would ever be able to bank on anything. As she turned into Candlemaker Row it began to rain. She turned up her collar and wheeled her bike along the pavement. It was murder cycling on the cobbles. Fern always said you could buckle your wheels. On the bench near the end of the road a solitary tramp was sitting with a bottle on his knee. Claudia wheeled her bike right past his splayed feet before crossing the road and letting herself into the house. Fern made a point of crossing over much earlier. Sometimes, in a gang, the winos became nasty, barring the way and leaning over you. But generally they ignored children.

Claudia played her flute until Fern came home, going through her old books and picking out gloomy tunes while the rain trickled

23

down the pane. Fern had had a variety of occupations recently, none of them paying much or lasting long. Currently, she worked for an American couple, collecting their young children from the school and minding them till one or other of the parents came home from work. You couldn't call it a job, really. She was always picking up little pastimes like this from advertisements in the Post Office at the end of the street.

This evening, when she came in, Fern had Wilf Smee with her. Claudia glanced at him coldly and withdrew to her bedroom. Wilf Smee was Fern's latest. As far as Claudia could see, it was a totally lack-lustre relationship. Wilf was fuzzy-haired and pointy-nosed – an entirely unglamorous escort. Whenever Fern was preparing to go out with him, Claudia would arrive in her bedroom and perch on the end of her bed. '*Wilf Smee!* Why tart yourself up for Wilf Smee? . . . I hope to goodness my dad was a bit better-looking . . . not much of a sexpot, old Wilf, I shouldn't think. I shan't need to worry if you're late.' Fern kept her mouth shut. She made every effort to stop her ears too. Claudia's remarks could spoil an evening for her. There had been times, in the pictures or in restaurants, when she had remained an unthawed lump of misery for two or three hours. 'Does he know you're an easy lay?' Claudia would ask. 'Does he know you're a tramp? Does he know about me?'

This sort of talk had started up quite suddenly when Claudia was about twelve. Fern had been totally unprepared for it and had found no way of quelling it. As time had passed, and it had become more savage and more wounding, she had begun to consider it her just desert. She had sinned against Claudia by conceiving her in the first place and by keeping her after her birth. That was undoubtedly how Claudia felt. And she should be allowed to say so. If she wanted to blame Fern for their impoverished circumstances she had every right to do so.

Apart from Wilf, the only person to have an inkling of the ruthlessness of Claudia's onslaughts was Aunt Belle. She was Fern's sole surviving relative, her father's sister – and her confidante. 'A child needs to know what the limits are,' Aunt Belle said. 'You make a mistake, letting her talk to you like that. She's saying things you'll never forget, either of you. She's saying things you'll both begin to believe.' But Fern was convinced that it was like lancing a boil – you had to let the badness out.

Wilf stayed until a quarter past eleven, his usual time of departure. As the front door banged, Claudia came to the top of the stairs. 'He's gone,' called Fern. 'Do you want something to eat?'

Claudia came downstairs and dragged a stool up to the kitchen table. 'Wonder why he always goes away so early. D'you think it's your reputation he's worried about, or his own?'

At school, things began to shape very much as Claudia had foreseen. Sometimes she and Anna seemed the mainstay of the threesome, with Sylvie as hanger-on, and sometimes it was the others who seemed close and she felt the outsider. But, bit by bit, she managed to manipulate things so that she could be assured of always being in demand, while Sylvie and Anna began to take it in turns to be her chief friend for the day.

Sylvie didn't complain. To her, this state of affairs did not represent a drop in status. But Anna resented the change deeply. On days when she had felt out of things she would push a note into Claudia's hand as they were leaving school, or, if her mother slipped out, she would ring Claudia at home. 'You've ignored me all day. I loathe this set-up. I've tried to be nice but all I get is the two of you ganging up. I can't stand it when you both go on about what you've been doing at her house.'

'Well, you've been there yourself. You know what we're talking about.'

'You go all the time. You never seem to come here any more.'

'You never ask me.'

'It's Mum, she won't let me ask you. She says if you come here then I'll be asked back to your house and she doesn't like me coming down your street.'

'Thanks very much.'

'It's not me, Cloddie. It's her. You know what she's like.'

'You weren't very keen on coming here youself, though, were you?'

'I was. I loved it when we were actually inside. What does Sylvie think of it?'

'She hasn't been yet, as you know perfectly well.'

Quite deliberately Claudia hadn't asked Sylvie home. She'd explained that the house was tiny and lacking a garden. Sylvie hadn't minded. She knew what town houses were like, she said. She'd been glad to get away from London. And if Claudia liked coming out to East Edge, that was fine.

Towards the end of October, Aunt Belle wrote to Claudia and Anna, inviting them to spend half-term at Tod Pool. She could collect them from the bus station in Cranwick as before, she said, and drive them out to Tod's in her car. She would build Anna up to gigantic proportions this time. There would be no relapse.

As far as Claudia was concerned, there was nothing unusual or unexpected about the invitation. She visited Tod's five or six times a year and had been doing so ever since she could remember. It was one of the ways Belle tried to make Fern's life easier, that was all. Fern cast an eye over the letter at breakfast time. 'Fine,' she murmured. 'It'll mean I can go up to the OU course in Edinburgh.'

'She's asking Anna too.'

'So I see. You liked that in the summer, didn't you?'

'It was OK.'

'What's wrong, then?'

Claudia shrugged. She'd been hoping that somehow or other Belle wouldn't be able to have her. She'd been hoping to spend days on end at East Edge with Sylvie. The Lamonts' basement was being converted into a den for the children. There was a sitting-room with old rugs and sofas and a portable television. Next door was a kitchen and a broom cupboard that was being turned into a tiny cloakroom. Visitors would approach by way of steps outside and enter through a glass door. There would be no need to go through the main house at all.

'I think you're a bit ungrateful,' said Fern. 'Belle'd be terribly hurt. If you're thinking you're going to miss out on the fun and games at Sylvie's, I can tell you it's probably just as well. I hate

26

to think what a crowd of teenage boys will get up to, let loose on their own. I'm quite glad you'll be out of it.'

'The Lamont boys aren't like that. The parents will be upstairs all the time anyway. They aren't going to keep sticking their noses in, that's all.'

'It'll be a shambles in no time. They'll get all sorts hanging on – kids with nowhere to go. There'll be smoking and drinking and all that sort of carry on. You're not old enough.'

A familiar cold gleam shone in Claudia's eye. 'Oh, I see. You're the prime example of how to behave, of course. The perfect model for any girl. I shan't go wrong if I follow in your footsteps.'

At school, Anna was gleeful. 'Mum's phoning your mum. Aunt Belle's invited me for half-term. The letter came this morning. I wrote to her, you know, when I was ill at the beginning of term. Mum's going to let me go.'

Claudia was tight-lipped. 'How odd. She hates you coming to my house, yet she's quite happy to send you to the back of beyond to stay with my aunt . . . Crazy, really. How does she know Tod Pool isn't a slum too?' She reached for Anna's letter. 'Well, well. Seems to have taken to you in a really big way. Eating out of your hand, I'd say.'

'It's because she lives by the sea. Mum thinks it's healthy. It's only because Candlemaker Row's right in the town centre. She thinks I get every germ that's going.'

Claudia turned to Sylvie. 'We live in filth,' she said. 'I really should have told you before. The place stinks.'

Fern solved it all – or rather, to give credit where it was due, Wilf Smee solved it all. He arrived at Candlemaker Row to find Fern in tears. Claudia was at the pictures with Jayne Hooley. Right in front of Anna and Sylvie she'd asked Jayne to go with her. No one in their right mind would ask Jayne Hooley to sit beside them in the pictures. She lived over a chip shop and smelt of cod. Anna and Sylvie had rightly construed this move of Claudia's as a slight to themselves. They'd wandered along the road together after school, scheming reprisals, concealing from one another the extent to which they wished Claudia back.

Claudia had had tea with Fern, swamping her in a deluge of complaint – she didn't want to go to Tod's; Anna had practically taken over the place, anyway; Aunt Belle wouldn't think half as much of Anna if she could hear her going on about Candlemaker Row; Sylvie was just as bad, gawping about the squalor of Claudia's surroundings, hugging tight her smug little thoughts about East Edge and her basement, never expressing any regret that Claudia might not be able to go there at half-term. 'They're horrible snobs,' Claudia muttered. 'It's because I haven't got a proper home.'

'No problem,' said Wilf calmly, listening to Fern's account of this. 'Get Belle to invite Sylvie as well. Then Claudia can't complain she's missing anything and she'll have someone to divert her if Belle and Anna make a fuss of one another.'

'She's got a nerve, objecting to that,' said Fern. 'She's never made any effort to be nice to Belle. Takes her completely for granted . . . I wonder if Sylvie *could* be tempted away from her wretched basement . . . I've already had Mrs Hypocritical Hackman on the phone, asking if I think it's too much of an imposition for Anna to go again, raving about sea air and all the wonderful things she's heard about Tod's and Belle. She's asked me round to tea to discuss it. I nearly asked her to come here instead. That would've fixed her!'

Claudia hailed Wilf's plan as totally brilliant. By the time she came back from Jayne's, clutching a parcel of chips, Fern had already confirmed it as a possibility with Aunt Belle. 'I'll ring Sylvie now,' said Claudia. 'She won't be in bed.' On the phone her voice became shrill with excitement. She jigged from side to side. Fern watched her. When she'd been small she'd jumped everywhere. 'Jumping for joy!' people had remarked. They'd never seen such a bubbly child.

In the classroom next day there was only one momentary dip in the level of Claudia's euphoria. This was early on, when she broke it to Anna that Sylvie would be accompanying them. 'I thought it would be just us,' whimpered Anna. 'I thought it'd be like it was in the summer. It won't be as good with Sylvie.'

'It'll be better,' said Claudia. 'You and Belle can play duets all day if you want. I won't be nagging you to do something with me all the time.'

Still Anna was doubtful. It wasn't what she'd hoped for. On the other hand, it had seemed yesterday as if no one would be going to Tod Pool. Better the threesome, she decided, than nothing at all.

3

Belle Spark was Fern's father's older sister, now in her late sixties, plump, with a dimpled face which belied her firmness of character. She lived in the large stone house that had been her family's home for generations, in the village of Stone Bore in Norfolk. This was Tod Pool. In the past, it was said, local foxes – tods – had frequented a small pond nearby, but there was no sign of water now, though foxes abounded. Belle and her brother had embarked upon their education at the village school and spent their holidays roaming the cliffs and beaches. Those were the long, happy years. Recently Belle had fallen into the way of thinking that the misfortunes that had dogged herself and her family since then were, in some way, a necessary corollary – as if, having been so happy for so long, it now behoved them to be sad.

Belle's father, like his father and grandfather before him, had been doctor in Stone Bore. In his day, Tod Pool had flourished. There had been a cleaner, a cook and a nanny. Belle's mother, in gumboots and felt hat, had tended the extensive garden single-handed, harvesting produce all the year round. But things were different now. Paint was flaking from the woodwork and gutter-ing, and areas of the garden were overrun with nettles and willow herb. Only half a dozen of the twisted old apple trees remained, flowering and fruiting as abundantly as ever. Belle was twisted now, too – the result of old injuries and increasing age. She could hardly manage the place, she said. But she'd keep it ticking over for Fern and Claudia. There would be nothing else to hand on.

Until middle age, Belle had been a school teacher in Cranwick. Her parents had been independent and stubborn, scorning her suggestion that she live at home to keep an eye on them. But after the 'tragedy' they had dwindled rapidly. They had become infirm and muddle-headed and Belle had taken early retirement to move back to Tod Pool permanently. Tod's was where she wanted to be, she insisted. It was no hardship. She had always meant to come home.

For members of the Spark family, all events could be categorized as being pre- or post-'tragedy'. Anything happy tended to be pre-, and everything post- seemed to be unlucky and, in some way, a result of that first horror. It had been a car crash. Belle had been driving out to Tod Pool from Cranwick one Sunday with her brother and sister-in-law, Fern's father and mother, to have lunch with her parents. In a lane near the house their car had run headlong into a stranded milk tanker. Fern's parents had died at once and Belle had sustained the multiple injuries from which she'd never fully recovered.

Fern had been in her first year at London University. After a time of mourning with her grandparents at Tod Pool she chose to return, but within weeks she had become pregnant with Claudia. She came back to Tod Pool two months before the birth and slipped off her coat in the sitting-room. Her grandparents noticed nothing. 'I'm going to keep it,' she announced flatly to Belle in the kitchen. 'I didn't try to get rid of it. When it's born I shall keep it.' She had never revealed the name of the baby's father. 'A student' was all she would say – somebody who had been kind when she'd gone back to London after the accident. He didn't know about the baby.

It was then that Belle had bought the little house in Ratfield, a town only miles from where Fern had been brought up. Belle insisted on paying every penny herself. Fern's father had speculated unsuccessfully all his life. He'd left nothing to speak of. Fern should invest what little there was, Belle said. There was the baby to think of. Fern was the nearest she'd ever get to having a child of her own. She would spend her money on Fern, and Fern could spend hers on the baby. The grandparents, far from expressing disapproval, seemed not to notice any irregularity in the situation. It was nice to think of another baby in the family, they mumbled. Something to cheer everyone up. Perhaps it would be a boy, to carry on the family name.

By the time of Claudia's birth, Fern had been settled in Candlemaker Row for almost three weeks. There had at first been the idea in her mind and Belle's that she would return to university at some stage, but after a year or two of looking after Claudia and combating her own and other people's attitudes to her situation, she lost the will and the confidence. Twelve and a half years passed before she met Wilf Smee, the chief librarian at Ratfield library. The Open University course was his idea. There was more to Wilf than his spiky frame and corkscrew hair, Aunt Belle decided. She had her fingers crossed for Wilf Smee.

They travelled on the seven-thirty bus from the depot the day after school broke up. They spread themselves out on the long back seat and no one came near them.

'What's all this?' said Sylvie, looking over Anna's baggage. 'You look as if you're off for six months.'

'Clothes and homework,' said Anna. She picked up her violin case from the floor and laid it along the seat beside her.

'*Homework!*'

'Ah!' said Claudia. 'You obviously aren't familiar with Mrs Hackman's idea of what holidays are for. Holidays are for boning up on everything under the sun while everyone else is idling about. Holidays are for doubling your amount of music practice. Holidays are for working flat out, aren't they, Anna?'

Anna nodded. 'Mind you,' she mumbled, 'Mum's right, if you think about it. We really don't do all that much at school, do we? You should see what Ralph gets through in a term. And Dad says they do much more at St Anthony's than we do.'

'I could believe that!' said Claudia. 'Specky worms. All they can do is read.'

'Seriously, Anna,' said Sylvie, 'how much time are you planning to spend working and scraping away at your *vile din*?'

'I promised I'd do at least an hour's work a day – and forty-five minutes each on violin and piano.'

'My God!' groaned Claudia. 'Two and a half hours. You can't expect us to hang around waiting for you.'

Anna shook her head. 'I didn't think you'd mind now you've got Sylvie too. I've absolutely promised Mum. And she'll know if I haven't got on with it – she's marked all the pages. She'll know I've been messing around if they aren't finished.'

'I bloody give up!' Claudia pushed past Anna to the end of the seat and stared moodily out of the window.

'It's not my fault,' Anna whispered to Sylvie. 'Mum gets worried if I'm not top in everything. She says it's only OK for them to be spending a fortune on Ralph's education if she can see I'm doing fine at home. If I start doing badly she'll get in an awful state.'

'Poor you.'

'She's been in Ratfield Royal. She was in for about six months. Claudia knows.'

'The mental hospital?'

Anna nodded. 'Dad says she's on a knife edge. He says she was all right before Ralph and I came along. It's the worry.'

'What's your dad like?'

'He's nice really. But he works all the time. We can't make a sound in the house because it disturbs him. I have to get all my practice done before he gets home, or while he's having his supper. I hardly ever have anybody round.'

'Look, Anna,' said Sylvie. 'You must try and come round to our house more often. The basement's going to be really good.'

'I'm not allowed out much.'

'Well, don't let Claudia ruin this, then. You know what she's like.'

'We've been best friends for eight years.'

The journey to Cranwick took three hours and six minutes. Claudia timed it. Aunt Belle was waiting at the bus station, bundled up in an old fur coat. She took them straight to a café for cream doughnuts and use of conveniences. She welcomed Sylvie and Anna as warmly as she did Claudia. 'You'd think we were nieces too, wouldn't you?' Anna whispered. 'Isn't she marvellous?' Claudia watched her great-aunt's hunched back as she stood at the counter loading a tray. There should have been a special sign that she was the blood-relative – the favoured one.

Aunt Belle's old blue car had lasted from her teaching days and she intended to run it till it dropped to bits. The girls tossed for

33

who should sit in front on the journey to Tod's and giggled as Belle, grunting under her breath, jogged out into the stream of traffic.

'You're in the suicide seat, Anna. If there's a crash you'll be crushed to pulp,' said Claudia from the back. She suspected Anna of rigging the result of the toss.

'I'd rather not hear talk of that sort, Cloddie,' said Aunt Belle quietly.

Claudia squirmed. How could she be expected to remember the tragedy all the time? She'd never known her grandparents. She couldn't be expected to think of them every time she got into a car.

Aunt Belle had left a casserole in the oven at Tod's. The smell of it filled the kitchen. Sylvie beamed. 'It's always like this,' said Anna. 'I love it.' She threw her arms round Aunt Belle's neck suddenly and kissed her. 'It's fantastic to be back!'

Aunt Belle looked pink and rather pleased, Claudia thought. Trust Anna to hit on the right thing to do. And trust it to be something Claudia would never have thought of. She'd never kissed Aunt Belle and couldn't start now.

That was just the beginning. From then on, all day, Anna became increasingly infuriating. Whatever they did, wherever they went, she chattered on tirelessly, introducing Tod's to Sylvie as if it were hers. 'Oh, wait till you see the garden!' she said while they were upstairs, deciding where to sleep. 'Wait till you see the beach.'

'You could do some of your homework,' said Claudia. 'I'll show Sylvie round. It doesn't need two.'

But Anna wouldn't be shaken off. She hurried ahead, pointing things out, telling anecdotes, all the time demonstrating to Sylvie that she had been here before and, to that extent at least, had the prior claim to Tod's. 'Isn't it great, showing it all to someone else?' she called over her shoulder to Claudia. 'It makes it new all over again. You must have felt like this when you showed me round in the summer.' Claudia didn't reply. Hatred was puffing up inside her like a giant balloon. Anna's every word and action inflated it to bursting point. She felt purple in the face.

After supper, they stayed on in the kitchen to do some baking. Aunt Belle had an electric stove as well as the Aga. There was no shortage of ovens. She supplied recipe books and ingredients and settled herself in an easy chair with a bottle of wine. She wasn't going to lift a finger, she said. When everything was in the oven, they could share her wine. 'We had it in the summer too,' Anna whispered to Sylvie. 'Mum would have a fit.'

In due course, they gathered round Aunt Belle with their glasses. 'How's your music, Anna? We must play some more duets.'

'Sylvie plays the clarinet,' said Claudia.

'But she hasn't brought it with her,' said Aunt Belle. 'Tut, tut! A bit like Claudia's flute, I expect. A much neglected instrument. What do you like doing best, Sylvie?'

'When we were in London, we used to go to galleries and plays and concerts and things like that. But now we've moved to the country I just like being out of doors.'

'Plenty of that here,' said Belle. 'And there might be something worth seeing in Cranwick. Any other special requests?'

'Just six days of being here with you,' said Anna, draining her glass. 'There couldn't be anything better than that.' For a wild moment Claudia visualized herself seizing the glass and grinding it into Anna's face. Belle was reaching past her with the bottle. Anna was giggling. 'I'm not allowed really!'

'Don't tell, then,' said Belle. 'A little does you no harm. It's better to experience these things gradually than to find yourself thrown in at the deep end one day.'

'That's what Dad thinks,' said Sylvie. 'We have it for lunch on Sundays. One of my brothers was sick once.'

Later that night, while the others were preparing for bed, Claudia sneaked back down the stairs and along the passage to the kitchen. Belle turned in surprise. She was sitting in her comfortable chair, reading by the light of a small lamp. 'I thought you were off to bed, Cloddie. I'm just having a nightcap.'

'I don't seem to have spoken to you properly – with the others being here.'

'It's lovely,' said Belle. 'I'm so glad you want to bring your friends.'

'It means I don't see so much of you, though. You have to spread yourself out over all three of us.'

Aunt Belle sipped at her glass thoughtfully. 'Isn't it strange, dear – in the back of my mind I was wondering if you found it all a bit dreary here with just me. I was wondering if that was why you'd started bringing friends.'

'Course not,' mumbled Claudia. 'I knew they'd like it, that's all.'

'I know you've sometimes had the feeling you were just being bundled off down here because your mother had something better to do.'

Claudia turned her blushing face to the floor and studied her feet. 'I've never minded coming. I just mind her sending me.'

'Fern's got to have a bit of a life of her own. She's only a girl. We've got to give her a chance.'

'She's not a girl at all. I'm the girl. What about my chance?'

Belle sighed. She patted the soft arm of her chair. 'Come and sit here. I know how you feel. But you're a little survivor compared with your mother. I've seen the way she dances to your tune. I know the hoops you put her through. She's only thirty-two, remember. She's got years ahead of her to plan for. That doesn't mean anybody's forgetting you.'

'She's still got that boy-friend,' grunted Claudia. 'The thin one. She sees him all the time.'

'I was going to ask about Wilf,' said Belle. 'How are you getting on with him?'

'I'm not. I clear off the minute he arrives. He's wet. Anyway, they don't want me around.'

'I don't suppose that's true.' Belle pushed herself up out of her chair and stood looking down at Claudia. 'Anyway, you've got good friends. I can see that. Try counting all the ways you're lucky. You've got Anna and Sylvie and a mother who's devoted to you – and me.' She took Claudia's hand and pulled her to her feet. 'I love you,' she said, wagging a finger. 'I always have, from the moment you came bawling your way into Number Nine.' She folded her arms right round Claudia and squeezed her tight. Claudia stood very still, arms pinned to her sides, aware of her molehill breasts in collision with Aunt Belle's mountainous ones. It must all be Anna's influence. Belle hadn't hugged her like this before. 'Up you go, now,' said Belle. 'I've got a hospital appointment in the morning. I don't want to be late to bed.'

Upstairs, Sylvie and Anna were sitting at the end of one of the beds, stripped to the waist. They were staring into a wide mirror on the dressing-table. 'What on earth's going on?' whispered Claudia from the door.

'Comparing tits,' giggled Anna. 'Aren't Sylvie's enormous?'

'What about Aunt Belle?'

'She won't come up. She doesn't care what we get up to. What's wrong, anyway?'

'One of mine's still a bit bigger than the other,' said Sylvie, peering at her reflection with narrowed eyes. 'It used to be much worse, you know. At my last school I hated changing for swimming. I thought everyone'd see.'

'Let's have a look at yours, Cloddie,' said Anna.

'Don't be stupid.' Claudia turned her back and undressed quickly, pulling on her pyjama top before anyone could see anything. Any changes in her body were her affair. Nobody else need comment or be concerned with them at all. She had firmly rejected Fern's offers of explanation. She knew the facts of life, she said. She'd known them for years. She knew exactly what Fern had been up to.

They lay on their backs in the narrow beds – two camp beds and the single that Belle had slept in as a child – and talked. Anna was explosively giggly and, in exasperation, Claudia feigned sleep. She rolled on her front, feeling the two points of growth on her chest sore and bruised against the mattress. She'd have to find some other sleeping position, she thought. What on earth size were they going to grow to? Anna and Sylvie were whispering about periods. Anna was gasping and asking endless questions. Claudia closed her eyes. Why did people enjoy getting in a huddle and talking like that? It would be just her luck if Anna and Sylvie became all pally and secretive, making her the odd one out here,

37

of all places. She thought about Belle. She'd seemed on Fern's side at first, but then there had been that huge hug. The kitchen had been warm and dark, smelling of their buns and cakes cooling on wire trays. When Claudia fell asleep, she dreamed that she and Belle had hollowed out a nest for themselves in the middle of a giant fresh-baked loaf, still warm from the oven.

4

Belle hummed as she made breakfast. 'Just a check-up,' she said. She'd been to the hospital before. She left the girls still in their dressing-gowns. Claudia hummed too, making toast for her friends and searching the cupboards for honey and marmalade. Anna and Sylvie had lost interest in their bodies now. At any rate they weren't talking about them any more. In fact, Anna seemed rather subdued and it wasn't long before a familiar pucker appeared on her brow and she began to look round for a quiet corner to settle with her books.

'I'm glad Anna's not coming,' Claudia whispered as she and Sylvie let themselves out of the back door. 'I've kept a few things to show you myself. I was sick of her yesterday.'

At the bottom of the garden, the grass was knee-high. 'You wouldn't know there's supposed to be a path here,' said Claudia. 'All this has grown up again since summer.' They beat their way towards an overgrown gate in the hedge and climbed over it, coming out on to a grassy knoll. 'Wait till you get to the top,' said Claudia, leading the way. 'We're still very sheltered here.' The cliffs were bare, wasted by winds from the open sea. They leaned forward, holding down their hoods and gasping for air. Sylvie tugged at Claudia's arm and signalled retreat, but Claudia battled forward. 'There's a path. You can't see it from here.' At the cliff edge, buffeted by the blast, they gazed down the rolling face. A little to their right, a track ran down into a thicket some yards below. This extended, in a wandering line, right down to the shingle beach. Claudia took Sylvie's hand and slithered forward.

The bushes were taller and thicker than they'd seemed from above, and closed over their heads as they squatted on their haunches. The track was worn deep into the cliffside so that Sylvie had the impression of having dropped, like Alice, into a big rabbit-hole.

'You can get all the way down to the beach,' said Claudia. 'There's a freak layer of soil. That's why the bushes keep growing. Their roots make the ground a bit more stable – otherwise we'd go slipping and sliding all the way down.' When they stood up, their heads poked out into the gale again. 'Let's crawl,' shouted Claudia. She dropped to her hands and knees and began to clamber downhill.

On the beach, a loose-limbed mongrel dog was gambolling in and out of the breakers. It shook itself dry and lolloped behind them as far as Hinton Warren, a three-mile stretch of sand and dunes, where they took the steps up from the beach to a cliff-top café. 'We've been ages,' said Sylvie as they sat down with crisps and tomato soup. 'What about Anna?'

'She's had peace for her homework. She won't mind. Anyway, she'd hate the wind. She's not as tough as us.'

The rain was just starting as Belle nosed the car up beside the house. It was a moment before she spotted Anna huddled in a corner amid a mass of screwed-up scraps of paper. 'I can't do it,' Anna wailed. 'There are answers in the back of the book and I can't get any of them right.'

'Where are the others?' asked Belle, unknotting a plastic rainhood. 'We'll never build you up if you carry on like this.' She gestured at Anna's books, spread over the floor. 'Put the whole lot away.'

'I promised Mum. She wouldn't have let me come otherwise. She likes me to get on.'

'Get ahead, you mean,' said Belle. 'She needs her head examined . . . No, no, I don't mean anything by that. I know your mother hasn't been well. But this isn't going to help, is it? I'll have to have a think over the next day or two.'

'I've got to do it,' Anna said. 'I promised.'

Claudia and Sylvie stopped on the doormat and looked at each other. Music was coming from the sitting-room. 'It's them,' said Claudia.

'Sounds like a flipping record.' Sylvie sat down on the floor and tugged at her boots. 'I didn't know Anna was that brilliant.'

'She pushed,' said Claudia. 'I told you that. Mum and Belle don't have a clue about my flute playing, you know. I like playing on my own, that's why. They hardly ever hear me. But Anna's mum listens to every note. She sits over her while she's practising.'

'You can tell she likes it, though. Just from the way she's playing. You can't force people to like things. You can't play that well unless you've really got it inside.'

'Oh,' said Claudia. 'Perhaps I should scrap my flute lessons.'

Sylvie glanced up. 'Don't be silly. Just because Anna's musical doesn't mean you're not. I'm musical too, but I could never play like that. Of course the amount of practice she does makes a big difference. I'm just saying she's not completely mechanical, that's all.'

'Oh,' said Claudia. She lined their boots up by the back door and turned to Sylvie with a bright smile. 'Of course she's not mechanical. She's fantastically good.'

A log fire burned in the sitting-room. Flames shone in the dark wood of the upright piano. 'Sit yourself down,' said Belle through the music. 'We shan't be long.' Claudia and Sylvie sat, back to back, on the rug in front of the fire, their cheeks burning, heads heavy.

'What was that?' said Sylvie drowsily as Anna put down her violin.

'Handel,' said Anna. 'I've got the Largo to learn. I know the other movements already.'

'What happened at the hospital, Aunt Belle?' said Claudia.

'Not a lot. Hardly worth the bother of going.' Belle got up stiffly and hobbled to the door. 'Bit of cold in my joints.'

Claudia followed her into the kitchen. 'Is it your arthritis?'

'Don't pester.' Belle limped to the sink and filled a kettle. 'It's none of your business, is it?' Claudia's face flamed. 'Oh, Cloddie!' said Belle. 'I'm sorry.' Once again her big arms folded round Claudia. 'Nothing's wrong, dear.'

After supper, they turned out every light in the house and sat round the fire telling ghost stories. Belle took whisky from a decanter and sank deep into her chair. She said very little and became very still, but, every now and then as she lifted it, her glass twinkled in the firelight. At midnight, when the girls switched on the light, she was fast asleep. They stood in a startled row, staring down at her. Her slippered feet were crossed at the ankle, her hands clasped, and her white head had dropped forward on her chest.

'We'd better just leave her,' whispered Claudia, putting a guard in front of the fire and removing Belle's glass.

Upstairs they undressed quietly and turned out the light. 'Do you think she could be ill?' whispered Anna. 'Fancy dropping off when we were making all that racket. You don't think she'd had heart failure or something?'

'My mother dozes in front of a fire like that,' said Sylvie. 'She's probably finding us a bit tiring.'

'We're trying to help,' said Anna. 'We're doing our beds and washing the dishes.'

'She drank a hell of a lot of whisky tonight,' said Sylvie. 'Did you notice? She was really knocking them back.'

'Are you trying to say she's drunk?' said Anna. 'I think that's really mean, Sylvie.'

'Mr and Mrs Hackman are TT,' sniggered Claudia. 'Never a drop in the house. Anna's the big soak of the family, aren't you, Anna?'

Downstairs a door opened and footsteps shuffled along the passage to the kitchen. 'Not dead, anyway,' giggled Claudia. 'Just dead drunk.'

The last days were calm and unseasonably warm. The girls trudged the stony beach for hours or lined up pieces of flotsam along the breakwaters and competed to knock them down with pebbles. Usually they took cheese and fruit with them, but sometimes they ended up in the café at Hinton Warren. 'How's your aunt?' the proprietor asked Claudia one day. 'I heard she wasn't so well.'

'She hasn't said anything to us.'

'Course she has,' said Sylvie. 'There was that hospital appointment.'

'Hospital now, is it?'

'No, it's not,' said Claudia. 'She's fine.'

'You didn't need to bite his head off,' whispered Anna as the man turned away. 'He was only being kind.'

'What's it got to do with him?' snapped Claudia. 'You won't get me coming in here again.'

Sylvie was gazing out of the window. 'I wonder why Belle never married,' she murmured. 'You'd think she'd have been really popular.'

'She was,' said Claudia. 'She married an airman in the war. He was called David Tattersall. He was killed. They hardly had any time together. He must've been about the last casualty, Mum says.'

'She should be Mrs Tattersall, then,' said Anna.

'She changed her name back after he died. Apparently she used to say she hadn't had time to get used to anything else anyway. She never mentions David Tattersall – not ever.'

'Perhaps she's got a photo in a secret locket, or something,' said Sylvie.

They finished their soup in silence. 'She suddenly seems quite different to me,' said Sylvie picking at the crumbs on her plate. 'I thought she was a spinster. You know . . . I thought she hadn't had anything to do with men.'

'She hasn't,' said Claudia. 'He died about forty years ago.'

'Still, he was around for a bit.'

'He was away in the war.'

'Still, at least they had a wedding night.'

'Oh, Sylvie – shut up,' said Anna, beginning to laugh and go pink.

'I don't suppose she's a virgin, if that's what you mean,' said Claudia. 'But I bet she can't remember anything about it.'

'*Shut up*,' said Anna, giggling furiously. 'I won't be able to look her in the face. You can't go on like that about someone like Aunt Belle.'

'Why not?' said Sylvie. 'It's perfectly natural. I could go on like that about anyone . . .'

'So could I,' agreed Claudia. She began to reel off the names of school teachers. 'Mrs Simmonds, Mr Ackroyd, Mr Aspel, Mrs

43

Cribbins, Mr Carpenter . . .' Anna was becoming purple in the face and cramming her hand across her mouth. 'Sylvie's mum and dad, your mum and dad . . .'

'*Your mum*!' Anna shrieked. Her voice rang round the room. The man stared across from his counter as Claudia snatched up her anorak and strode out.

Back at the house, Claudia was in the kitchen with Aunt Belle. They were listening to a play on the radio and taking it in turns to do everyone's ironing. 'Don't say a word,' Sylvie whispered to Anna as they stood in the doorway. 'She's going to pretend nothing's happened. I told you she'd be OK.'

At supper, Aunt Belle passed round a big brown bottle of cider. 'Homework time, Anna,' she called out suddenly at the end of the meal. 'Go and get your books.'

'*Now*!' said Anna. Her anxiety about the unfinished work had been mounting, but she had found herself almost as reluctant to rouse Belle's disapproval as her mother's. 'I thought you didn't want me to do it.'

'Now,' said Belle firmly. 'We're all going to do it. You've done your music practice. Nobody could do that for you. But now we'll all lend a hand with the rest.'

Anna made her way slowly upstairs. Were they all half drunk? Did they really think Mrs Hackman would see the funny side of this? She examined herself in the mirror. She looked the same as usual, but Mrs Hackman said that was the nasty thing about alcohol. It sneaked into your bloodstream without your noticing it. Claudia and Sylvie had come out into the hall. 'Get a move on, Anna,' they were calling.

For the next hour, the kitchen became very still. Belle's cat nosed curiously at people's feet, and purred, but nobody stroked him. Sylvie was reading a chapter on photosynthesis and making notes for Anna to learn on the way home. Claudia was writing an essay in painstakingly forged handwriting and Anna was doing her own maths. At half-past nine Belle swept all the books into a pile and bustled everyone out to the car.

'Where are we going?'

'Tarbridge.'

'Trashy Tarbridge!'

Tarbridge was for tourists – 'common', Mrs Hackman would have said. Coloured lights zig-zagged the length of the promenade and pop music blared from the arcades. Belle bought chips for everyone and brushed aside Anna's confession that she wasn't allowed to eat in the street. At the fun-fair they rode on the Bone Shaker and the Waltzers. Sylvie and Claudia queued for the Big Wheel, which eventually stranded them up at the top, swaying above the general hubbub. Claudia stared at a squeaking joint over her head and clutched Sylvie's arm. 'This thing's dropping to bits.'

'Look at Anna and Aunt Belle,' said Sylvie, leaning over the side. 'It's rather nice how well they get on, isn't it? Aunt Belle must like one of us actually choosing to stay with her half the time. Wonder what they're whispering about now.'

Claudia gazed giddily down to the ground, searching out the white and dark heads. 'Couldn't care less. They're both boring as hell.' The wheel was turning again, spinning them down past lights and grinning faces, then tossing them sky-high again.

Twenty-four hours later, they were once more suspended – in balcony seats above the stage of the Playhouse in Cranwick. Aunt Belle had bought tickets for *The Importance of Being Ernest* as a last night treat and, afterwards, she took them for a late meal in the theatre restaurant. At home, while they were all drinking Horlicks round the Aga, Anna began to sob. She'd remember the holiday for ever, she said, tears pouring down her face.

'We all will,' said Claudia. 'You don't need to fuss.'

Later, Claudia stole downstairs again in her dressing-gown. The kitchen was empty. She picked her way back across the dark hall and had reached the foot of the stairs when the door of the downstairs bathroom opened and Belle came out, also clad in a dressing-gown. She peered into the shadows, startled and puffy in the harsh light from overhead.

'Are you OK?' whispered Claudia.

'Oh, it's you, Cloddie. Nothing to worry about. I'll be all right when I lie down.' Belle switched off the light and padded off towards her downstairs bedroom.

Claudia stood there, watching her go. If she were Anna, of course, she'd be dashing down the passage after Aunt Belle, talking a lot of nonsense, making a big commotion. Belle had shuffled as far as her bedroom door. She was going in and closing it behind her. Claudia began to climb the stairs. Belle might at least have asked why she'd come down. She couldn't suddenly be *that* ill.

'Where've you been?' Anna and Sylvie were sitting bolt upright in the dark.

'Seeing Aunt Belle.'

'Oh, I wish you'd said,' said Anna. 'I'd have come too.'

'She's my aunt.'

'You haven't got secrets about us, have you?'

'You're not family, Anna,' said Sylvie. 'You've got to let Claudia and Aunt Belle get together once in a while. I think Belle's been marvellous the way she's treated us just like nieces too, but Claudia's the only Spark. It's only right if she gets a bit of extra attention.'

'I haven't, anyway,' said Claudia. 'You don't have to eat your heart out. She was going to bed. We didn't talk at all.'

5

'How was Tod Pool?' said Wilf Smee. He'd arrived early on the Wednesday evening of the following week to take Fern to a concert.

Claudia shrugged. 'Same as usual.'

'That doesn't mean a lot to me, of course,' said Wilf good-naturedly. 'Never having been.'

'You must get Mum to take you. She likes fixing up for outsiders to invade the place.' Claudia picked up her school-bag and walked past him into the hall.

'I've brought some new books from the library,' called Wilf. 'I'd like your opinion. It's hard to know what to order these days.' There was silence from the hall. Wilf opened his briefcase, took out three or four novels and stacked them in a corner. She was bright, Fern had said. There must be some way of getting through to her. Through the window he caught sight of Fern scurrying down the road, coat flapping. She looked frail and agitated. He wanted to throw up the window and shout, 'You don't have to rush for me – I won't go away.'

Claudia had been foul-tempered all day. Anna had started it, bursting into the classroom at nine o'clock, waving a letter from Aunt Belle. 'I wrote as soon as we got back. She's replied by return!'

'God!' said Sylvie. 'I haven't written at all.'

'Mum phoned,' Claudia grunted. 'I spoke to her then.'

'She sent Mum a note too,' said Anna. 'She said she really enjoyed the week and Mum must send me any time she wants – for sea air. Mum's bought her a box of herb soap. She's sending it off today.'

'When are you thinking of going again, then?' said Claudia. 'I wouldn't want to barge in on any arrangement you'd made with my aunt.'

'Oh, I wouldn't go without you,' said Anna. 'Don't be silly. She just means I can come any time you're going. I thought you'd be pleased. I thought you found it boring going on your own. I thought that was why you asked me in the first place.'

At break and lunchtime Claudia hissed abrupt comments and messages in Sylvie's ear. 'What the hell gives her the right to take over Tod's? . . . Why can't Aunt Belle see what a pain she is? . . . What about us?' Anna hung in the background. At the end of school, she ran up and said that, if they wanted, she'd never go back to Tod Pool again, no matter how pressing Aunt Belle's invitations. 'It's only because she's sorry for me being ill all the time. She's not asking me because she likes me best or anything like that.'

'Bloody right!' snapped Claudia. She jumped on her bike and pedalled off. At the end of the road she waited for Sylvie to catch her up. They were going out to East Edge. The basement was completely finished, and Jack and Raymond had had all their friends round at half-term. Claudia was to be Sylvie's first guest. They were going to have tomato soup, sausages and baked beans for tea and do their homework together.

Sylvie was a long time coming. She pulled up beside Claudia, flustered and red in the face. 'You've been a bit of a pig, you know. She's in tears back there. Why do you go for her all the time? She has a horrible life. She'll be practising her music while we're making our supper. And then there'll be extra homework laid on by her mother over and above the normal stuff. I invited her today too, you know. But her flipping mother wouldn't let her come, of course. I wanted both of you.'

Claudia's face twisted into a grim smile. 'I'm so sorry she can't come, Sylvie. I'm sorry your evening's obviously going to be one big flop. Perhaps it'll improve matters if I don't come either.'

She turned her bike round with a jerk and jumped on to it. As she rode away she cocked an ear for Sylvie's voice. But there was no sound from behind, and when she reached the corner and glanced back, Sylvie had gone.

*

So here she was, home at Number Nine with Wilf Smee, and nothing in the fridge for supper. Downstairs the door banged as Fern came in. There was a mumble of voices, then Fern calling. 'Cloddie, I thought you were out this evening. What about your tea?' Claudia didn't reply. '*Claudia*!' Let the old cow bloody well come up. Mean pig, expecting anyone to go into details about rows with friends in front of that pinhead boy-friend. Fern bounded up the narrow stairs and poked her head round the door. Claudia was stretched out on her bed, arms behind her head. 'Why aren't you at Sylvie's? There's no tea here. Wilf and I are eating out. Can you make do with an egg?'

'Charming! Dinner for you two in some cosy little joint and an egg for me. Great!'

'I thought you were going out for tea.'

'Cancelled.'

'Why?'

'Sylvie makes me sick most of the time.'

'Oh dear,' said Fern. 'You've had a row. Well, there's bread and some eggs and tins of beans and things. Could you manage with those and I'll bring you in some chips or something?'

'Don't bring anything from Hooleys'. I'd throw up. Off you go and have a really wonderful time.'

Fern fidgeted in the doorway. 'Well, I will have to go, Cloddie. We're meeting friends of Wilf's. It's a foursome.'

Claudia flicked open the cover of a book. 'Well, off you go then. What's keeping you?'

Fern sighed and pulled the door behind her. 'Rotten start to the evening, as usual,' she muttered at Wilf in the hall. 'I hate leaving her in that sort of mood.'

Wilf glanced upstairs to the dark landing. 'Come here,' he whispered, seizing Fern suddenly. 'What that little bitch needs is a man about the place. You know that, don't you?'

Fern wriggled. 'Don't, Wilf. She'll see.'

'What if she does? It's time she knew.'

'She knows quite enough, as a matter of fact.'

Claudia sat up as the front door banged, and rushed to the window. For a moment she could just see Fern and Wilf setting off up the Row. Wilf was making a point of walking on the road side. Claudia focused on his pointed curly head. 'Bloody idiot!' she muttered. In the living-room, she lit the gas fire and got out her flute. Miss Matchett had been impressed last lesson. She'd looked hard at Claudia and said she was suddenly playing with maturity. It was exciting, she'd said. At home, Claudia usually practised alone. She felt ridiculous with Fern in the room and preferred to play with absolutely no expression at all rather than run the risk of Fern saying, as she once had, 'That was beautiful, Cloddie. I could really hear you feeling that. It really got to me.' The notion of involving Fern in her feelings gave Claudia the creeps. In fact, the idea of closeness with anyone induced a slight queasiness these days. Even the bond with Anna, which had always been easy to live with, being unselfconscious and largely unspoken, had become uncomfortable now that Anna was so possessive of her and fearful of losing her to Sylvie.

It took Sylvie almost an hour to decide whether or not to risk it. She dithered at the end of Candlemaker Row, holding half a pound of sausages, moving aside for a wiry little man and his blonde companion to hurry past. She knew Claudia hadn't really wanted her to come home. Would she be awfully angry at being tracked down? It was dark by the time she chained her bike to a lamp-post and made her way down the street on foot. Ahead of her, a drunk in a long raincoat lurched on and off the pavement. The Row was longer than it had looked from the main road; it curved gently to the left until you couldn't see where you'd come from – only the black walls on either side and cracked windows. Sylvie's heart pounded. A door might open at any moment and a hand come out to grab her. No one would ever know she'd been here. Ahead of her, the tramp suddenly veered over the road to a bench under a street-lamp on the other side. Sylvie glanced again at the street numbers.

One window was dimly lit. A square of light fell on the pavement ahead and Sylvie glanced in as she passed. In the middle of a small room Claudia was swaying to and fro in front of a music stand, her flute to her lips, her eyes closed. Sylvie pressed up to the window and listened till the piece was finished, then she tapped lightly on the glass. A moment later the street door opened and Claudia jumped outside. '*Sylvie*! I nearly had a heart attack. I thought you were one of that lot.' She pointed at the tramp.

'Is your mum in?' said Sylvie. 'I've brought some sausages. I thought we could have them here.'

'No one's here,' said Claudia. 'Mum's out with her boy-friend.'

In Claudia's kitchen they made the exact meal they had been planning to have in Sylvie's basement and carried it through to the living-room to eat by the gas fire. Claudia turned off the lamp and lit the big square candles at either end of the mantelpiece. 'What about your mum? Won't she be worried?'

'I saw Ray in town. I told him to say I was here. I've seen your address on your flute case. I hope you don't mind.'

'Not if you don't. I hope your mum won't either. Not like Mrs Hackman.'

'No, she won't mind. Anna doesn't either, you know. She can't help the parents she's got.'

'She takes after them in lots of ways. She hates this street. She can't see anything good about it. Actually, it's very special historically. It's on a list of places to be preserved.'

'I don't think Anna knows what she thinks half the time. She's desperate to please her parents, that's all – and desperate to have you as a friend and, after that, me.'

'Oh, I know,' mumbled Claudia. 'I shouldn't have been horrible to her. We've been friends for years. And I'm sorry I went for you too. I've been cursing myself for missing the chance of seeing your basement.'

She crossed to the window, looked out, then drew the curtains. 'Small, isn't it?' she said, spinning round and catching Sylvie looking quickly round the room. 'A mousehole compared with your place.'

They spread their homework over the floor and tested each other on French vocabulary and compared their maths answers. When Sylvie stood up to go she spotted a photograph of Fern on the mantelpiece. 'Is this your mum? She passed me in the street earlier on. She's really young, isn't she?'

Claudia nodded. 'The trouble with her is she's a bit of a tart. Still, I shouldn't complain. If she hadn't been, I wouldn't be here.'

They left the house together, linking arms as they stepped out in the dark. Sylvie found herself hurrying, but Claudia held her back. 'Slow down! What's the rush?'

'You don't sound as if you like your mum very much,' whispered Sylvie. 'It must be difficult having no father. Don't you ever get used to it? Some of the things you say are very odd.'

Claudia didn't answer for a long time. Sylvie began to count their footsteps. They turned the bend and the main road was in sight.

'You'd be odd,' said Claudia, 'if you were me. My mum's had more blokes in her time than yours has had hot dinners. I'd rather have just about anybody else's mum – barring obvious exceptions like Jayne Hooley's. I'd even rather have Mrs Hackman and that's saying something.'

Sylvie felt her stomach twisting into a tight knot. Absolutely nothing was sacred to Claudia. She seemed to have no basic loyalties at all. – She wasn't normal.

'What's wrong?' said Claudia. Sylvie had stopped speaking as they came to the end of the Row. She was crouching down now, undoing the padlock on her bicycle chain.

Sylvie straightened up and forced herself to meet Claudia's eye. Claudia was looking puzzled, rather younger than usual, pulling at one of her tight curls. 'I wasn't expecting you to be so nasty about your own mother. But I can understand it.'

'Oh, I see,' said Claudia, turning away and waving as Sylvie wheeled her bike on to the road. 'See you tomorrow.' She made her way home, cat-footed, hugging the shadows. Sylvie had looked scared stiff. She obviously hadn't understood a thing. She was dumb.

That night Fern was ill. She came in with Wilf, complaining of a sick headache, and went straight to bed. Wilf stood in the living-room, twiddling his car keys and offering to sleep on the sofa.

'We've always looked after ourselves before,' Claudia said. 'We'll manage.' Wilf scribbled his phone number on a slip of paper and pressed it into Claudia's hand. 'We've got it,' she said. 'Mum spends half her life on the phone to you.'

Later she wished Wilf had stayed. Fern shuddered and talked gibberish. When Claudia made her a cup of tea at three in the morning, she knocked it away, splashing most of it over Claudia's bare feet. Claudia ran cold water into the bath and sat on the edge with her scalded toes submerged. What if Fern died? She shivered, watching her toes turning blue.

In the morning, the doctor came and wrote out a prescription for Fern. Wilf arrived with a bottle of Lucozade and freesias tied with a bow.

At first, it was quite dramatic dashing home from school to look after a sick mother but, by the end of a week, it was simply a drag. Fern's temperature rose and fell unpredictably. She was permanently on the mend but never mended. Every evening, Wilf turned up with a beautifully wrapped gift and tiptoed upstairs, whispering to Claudia that if Fern was asleep he'd just sit there – Claudia could forget about him. She found that impossible, though. Visions of his razor-sharp face hanging over Fern's pillow lurked constantly in the back of her mind. She found herself unable to concentrate on homework. She couldn't practise her flute. She couldn't even phone Anna or Sylvie for fear he'd be eavesdropping.

In the end, it was Anna, not Claudia, who was Sylvie's first guest at the basement. Sylvie phoned them both one Saturday with an invitation to spend all day at East Edge. 'Mum's not well again,' said Claudia. 'I think I'll have to stick around at home.'

'Get Wilf to stay with her,' said Sylvie. 'Do come. Mrs Hackman's even letting Anna out for the day! It's practically a miracle.'

'Is it hell!' grunted Claudia. 'She'd probably let Anna spend every day of the week with you. It's only slums and single-parent families she rules out.' She put down the phone. Later she did the weekend's shopping and poached a fillet of plaice for Fern, who then fell deeply asleep. Claudia did her homework till four o'clock, when Wilf arrived and crept upstairs as usual. All of a sudden, it seemed perfectly possible to escape. She slipped on her anorak and was wheeling her bike out into the street when Fern's bedroom door opened and Wilf came sneaking back down the stairs. 'You're not going out, are you?' he whispered. 'I just brought her a little present. I can't actually stay today.'

'I'm only going off for a couple of hours,' said Claudia, gripping her handlebars tightly. 'I shan't be gone long.'

'Poor old Fern. That's rotten. Saturday evening and nobody here, just as she's beginning to perk up a bit. Have you got to go? She's been awfully low. I'd stay myself but I simply can't tonight. She knows that. She was sure you were going to be here. She's planning to come down later.'

Claudia hauled her bike noisily back into the house and unzipped her jacket. 'Right you are, Wilf,' she said. 'I'll stay. I've stayed in for ages, fetching and carrying and being totally ignored. What's one more night?'

Wilf squeezed past her to the door. 'Jolly good,' he muttered. 'She hasn't meant to abandon you, you know. She's only tried to keep you out of her room because she was worried you'd catch her bug.'

'What about you? You're not telling me she doesn't care about you?'

It was two hours before Fern wobbled downstairs in her dressing-gown. 'I'm glad you're here,' she said, flopping on to the settee. 'Lucky nobody asked you anywhere.'

'They did. I could have been there and back twice over by now – only your bloody boy-friend said I had to stay in.' Fern's head drooped. 'Oh, marvellous!' groaned Claudia. 'Great company for a Saturday night!'

Fern returned to bed soon afterwards. When Claudia went up at ten o'clock there was no sign of light under her door. Claudia turned out her own light and lay in bed staring up at the ceiling. Why couldn't Wilf clear off? Nobody wanted him interfering. He was making Fern weedier and weedier. Ever since there had been Wilf Smee to lean on, she'd been keeling right over. Men weren't needed at Number Nine. Wilf wasn't a man anyway – more like a scratchy little twig. One of these days he'd snap in the middle and Fern would fall flat on her face.

*

Things had gone no more smoothly that evening for Anna and Sylvie at East Edge. They had pottered in the basement, unable to settle to anything for wondering if Claudia was coming or not. At tea-time they had made themselves a shrivelled meal on one of the electric rings in the tiny kitchen and listened to some records of Jack's. Later, Dr and Mrs Lamont had gone off in the car and Sylvie had brought out a box of her mother's discarded make-up and a couple of hand mirrors. Anna had looked on anxiously as she painted her eyes. 'Will it come off?'

'Stop being such a worry-guts. Here, close your eyes.' Sylvie had begun to stroke her brush boldly across Anna's eyelids.

They had worked away at their faces for a long time, progressing from subtle highlights to ludicrous daubing. They were giggling helplessly at each other when suddenly there was a rush of heavy footsteps down the steps outside and they turned to see half a dozen pupils from Ratfield Boys' crowding up against the glass door. Sylvie opened it a crack and peered out into the dark and cold. 'Jack and Ray aren't back from football yet.'

'They said we could wait.' The boys pushed their way past her. Anna scrambled about on the floor between their feet, gathering up lipsticks and eyebrow pencils. 'You two look a real pair of tarts!' said one of the boys. The rest laughed loudly. They were sprawling over the chairs, popping open cans of lager. One or two were lighting up cigarettes, flicking spent matches into the air.

Anna eventually shrank into a corner and scrubbed at her face with a hanky, but Sylvie tried to be hospitable. By the time Jack parked his bicycle against the wall and came racing down the steps, she was squeezed up on the sofa with a can in one hand and a cigarette in the other.

'Bloody hell!' shouted Jack from the door. 'Who said you lot could come?'

'Ray did. Ray lets us do anything.'

'Ray's great. We're waiting for Ray.'

Jack didn't say another word. As Anna told Claudia over the phone the next day, he just seemed to leap into the room and attack the whole lot of them at once. Ten minutes later the place was empty and Sylvie was getting a lecture. 'It's awful,' Anna said.

'Jack told us Raymond gets bullied at school. These boys weren't his friends at all. They'd just heard about the basement and decided to barge in. I was scared stiff.'

'What about Sylvie?'

'She kept thinking they were friends of Jack and Ray, so she tried to join in with them a bit. She felt sick after. Jack said it served her right. And we were sitting there with all that wild make-up on the whole time – like a pair of punks!'

'Dr and Mrs Lamont'll make a fuss.'

'Jack made us promise not to tell them. He said they might close the basement. And it's brilliant, Clod. It really is.'

'Mmmm,' Claudia grunted. She lowered her voice to a whisper. 'You've no idea the kind of weekend I've been having. Wilf couldn't stay yesterday, but he's been here practically all day today. Mum's supposed to be at death's door but he's been up in her room for hours. The bed keeps creaking – sounds as if it's about to crash through the ceiling. How on earth do they expect me to do my homework, I'd like to know!'

Anna giggled. 'Don't be an idiot, Clod. They can't be doing anything like that. I thought she'd got a raging temperature.'

'Red hot passion,' whispered Claudia. 'Sexual delirium! I'm just hoping Wilf's proving a bit of a disappointment. Then she might get rid of him.'

6

One snowy December afternoon, Claudia came skidding along the
Row after school to find Belle's car parked outside the house. She
raced the last few yards. Belle was standing by the gas fire in the
living-room, still clad in her coat, rubbing her hands together. Her
cheeks were pinched, the split veins blue beneath the white skin.
'You look frozen, Aunt Belle. We didn't know you were coming,'
said Claudia. 'I'll make a cup of tea.'

Belle followed her into the kitchen. 'Good job I've got my own
key to this place. I thought Fern would be here.'

'She's still at work. She looks after some little kids after school
– till their mum gets in. She won't be long. Are you staying? Have
you come for something special?'

Belle shook her head. 'I just want a word with Fern. Nothing
exciting.'

'Fancy driving in this weather,' said Claudia. 'It must be
important.'

'No,' said Belle firmly. 'Actually I'm escaping. Burst pipes.
Workmen all over the place.'

They sat down by the fire and gradually Belle's face turned pink
again. Claudia was relieved. She hadn't seen Belle like that before
– chilled through and frail. Belle was the one who kept everything
going. She didn't weaken or grow old. She'd always been white-
haired and lame but those weren't signs of weakness – they were
just aspects of Belle. 'Anna and Sylvie would love to see you. I
must give them a ring.'

'I'm definitely going to call on the Hackmans,' said Belle. 'I
want them to know Anna's in good hands when she comes to
Tod's. Mrs Hackman sounds so anxious on the phone. I'm sure
she hates not knowing exactly what I'm like.'

'Beggars can't be choosers,' muttered Claudia. 'As a matter of
fact, it's a wonder she ever let Anna come to Tod's in the first

place. She's really snobby. She doesn't like her coming here one bit.'

'The Tod visits are purely for the good of Anna's health,' said Belle. 'Mrs Hackman has been perfectly honest about that. They've got a son away at school and they can't afford holidays. I think it's very sensible of them.'

'All that homework's a bit crazy, though, isn't it? You must've thought so or you wouldn't have made a game of it.'

'They're over-anxious. Anybody might be with a daughter like Anna. She's so bright and talented, but highly strung and not very strong. A tremendous worry.'

Claudia sipped at her tea. 'Do you ever worry about me? I'd've thought there was loads more to worry about in my case.'

'I think about you a lot. But I don't worry. You're a survivor, I tell you.'

'Well, I wish I wasn't. I'd like someone to worry themselves sick about me for once.'

Belle got up stiffly to carry her cup back to the kitchen. As she passed Claudia she stopped and laid a hand on her head. 'I *count* on you. Do you know that? You're my one big hope,' she whispered. Her touch was electric. Claudia's scalp tingled. She sat rigidly still, unable even to look up. She had wanted Belle to humour her – to say she worried about her as much as Anna and loved her more. But now she could feel a trembling in Belle's fingers. Something odd was going on. Belle was drawing strength from *her*. The whole world was turning a slow somersault.

The front door opened and Fern came in with Wilf. Later, she and Belle shut themselves up in the kitchen to make supper and Wilf sat down in one of the wicker chairs opposite Claudia. He clasped his hands round his knees. 'Would you think I was just making conversation if I asked what kind of a day you've had at school?' he asked.

Claudia stared at him in surprise. 'What?'

Wilf began to rock backwards and forwards, staring beadily back at her. 'I was just making enquiries as to the sort of day you've had.'

'Fine, thanks.'

'I've got some more books in my bag. Do you want to look them over for me?'

The kitchen door opened and Fern's head popped round. Beyond, Belle was just visible leaning over the stove. 'You two all right?'

'Certainly,' said Wilf. As Fern's face disappeared, he opened his briefcase. 'Will you read these for me?'

'Do you intend to marry my mother?' whispered Claudia. 'Or is she just some sort of diversion for you?'

Wilf gave no sign of having heard her. He pulled four new books from his case and spread them over the floor. 'There,' he said. 'No hurry. Just let me know your opinions when you've formed them. – About the other,' he added. 'Yes – and – No.'

Claudia slipped on to the floor and gathered up the book. What did he mean, 'Yes – and – No' like that? She looked up. He was smiling. What did he mean, 'Yes – and – No'?

Upstairs, she sat shakily on the edge of her bed. She hadn't really expected him to reply. She'd only half intended him to hear her question in the first place. Do you intend to marry my mother? – *Yes.* Or is she just some sort of diversion? – *No.* That must be it. He couldn't mean anything else. Or was he just outbluffing her? She'd wanted to embarrass the life out of him. Perhaps he was just getting his own back. Fern would have said if things had got that serious. Anyway, even she would never be so insane as to marry Wilf. Imagine him in your bed every night. Claudia caught sight of her horrified face in the mirror. If Fern married Wilf, he'd be her own stepfather! . . . But she'd refuse to live with them. They couldn't force her. They wouldn't want her anyway. She'd move to Tod's permanently.

Claudia stayed upstairs till supper time, planning to catch Aunt Belle alone. Belle would sort it all out. She would know what was going on. At supper, they sat, all four, round the pine table in the warmly lit kitchen. 'Goulash!' purred Wilf. 'And wine! What a treat!'

'Don't waste any wine on Cloddie, Wilf,' said Fern, whisking Claudia's glass away. 'Who set a glass for her, anyway? She's too young.'

'Rubbish!' said Wilf. 'One glass won't do any harm. I bet she's had it before, haven't you, Claudia?'

'If she hasn't, it's high time she had,' said Belle with a wink.

The glass was replaced and filled. 'I'm just a weakling,' sighed Fern. 'She's my daughter. I should stick to my guns.'

Claudia took a sip of the wine. It was red and fruity. 'See, she likes it,' said Wilf. He was watching her closely. 'That's my girl!'

Throughout Belle's stay, there was an air of secrecy about the house – not of the exciting, tingling variety, but of the sort that brings dread and foreboding. For once, Wilf stayed away. Belle and Fern sat in the living-room murmuring in low, intent voices. When Claudia came in from school they gave little starts and tried to smile. Fern looked nervous. She *is* going to marry Wilf, Claudia thought. She's telling Belle but they daren't tell me. She loitered on the stairs, trying to catch Belle on her own, wondering if she could bring herself to ask. There must not be a wedding. It would have to be stopped. Not that she herself particularly wanted Fern, but Fern was all she'd got. She'd been cheated out of a father. But she had got a mother, however feeble and useless. And Fern could jolly well make a decent job of mothering her – which didn't include laying on stepfathers like Wilf Smee.

Mrs Hackman carried her tray of tea-things into the sitting-room and set it down on a low table beside Aunt Belle. They had been talking for almost an hour. Belle, still bundled in her coat and boots, had been nodding her cotton-wool head most sympathetically as she listened to Mrs Hackman's tales of woe. Mrs Hackman had gone off to boil the kettle with her cheeks flaming and her eyes bright. How extraordinary that this gentle old lady should be related to trollopy Fern Spark!

Aunt Belle loosened her coat as Mrs Hackman began to pour the tea through a silver strainer into bone china cups. 'We've got some nice things,' said Mrs Hackman. 'Mainly handed down from grandparents. And we're rich in our children, of course. That's what I always feel. It's just up to us to see they make the most of themselves. Naturally, one would expect to make sacrifices . . .'

'There have to be holidays,' said Belle, interrupting Mrs

Hackman's flow for the first time. 'And that's where I think I can help. I want you to feel free to send Anna down to Tod's whenever seems appropriate to you. I'll always be glad to see her. I want you to know that. I enjoy her company. I shan't consider it an imposition in any way.'

'I hate to feel I'm *taking* all the time,' said Mrs Hackman, perching on a small cane stool at Belle's side, her teacup on her knees.

'You're doing me a favour, I took to Anna at once. In character, she reminds me very much of my niece, Fern. Have you met Fern?'

Mrs Hackman nodded dumbly.

'She was a very bright little girl, delicate and artistic. My brother adored her. She's had a very tough time since her parents died – though things seem to be picking up now. There's a new young man . . .'

'Ah!' said Mrs Hackman, masking her astonishment that Aunt Belle should approve of the notion of 'new young men'. There had clearly already been at least one too many in the life of Fern Spark.

'She's just a girl herself, of course,' Belle was saying. 'She was only eighteen when Claudia was born. They've always been a couple of kids to me – growing up alongside. But Fern has matured a lot recently. Wilf Smee is a very steady chap, quite a bit older than Fern and very good with Claudia.'

'Oh, I see,' said Mrs Hackman. 'You think there will be wedding bells then? How wonderful for Claudia! A child is better off with two parents, I'm sure.'

'Quite,' said Belle. 'So you can see what Fern's been up against. Not a word to Anna, mind. It's by no means a settled thing.'

Mrs Hackman picked her way through the snow, following in Aunt Belle's boot-prints, to where the old blue car was parked against the kerb in front of the house. 'I expect Claudia will be coming to see me after Christmas,' said Belle as she climbed in. 'Send Anna too.'

Mrs Hackman shivered. 'The Christmas break is such a good time to catch up on a bit of homework.'

Aunt Belle was starting the engine. 'Take advantage of Tod's while you can. I shan't always be there.' She smiled and slammed the door. Mrs Hackman stood on the pavement in a cloud of fumes, watching the car out of sight. Was Belle planning a move? Perhaps she was coming to Ratfield to be near Fern and Claudia? It would obviously be sensible to take up the post-Christmas invitation in that case.

7

The basement at East Edge, festooned with paper-chains and Chinese lanterns, was due to come into its own during the Christmas holidays. On December the twenty-third, the Lamonts were going to hold a disco. Dr Lamont had agreed to buy tickets for himself and Mrs Lamont for a London show that night. He didn't want to stay at home, he said, being tempted to spy. He would form his assessment of the kind of party it had been from an inspection of the basement next morning. In the meantime, he ordered fifty small cans of beer and lager and Mrs Lamont promised a fruit punch. Admission should be by invitation only, they said, and the smuggling in of additional liquor strictly forbidden.

Sylvie handed out her invitations at school, a week before the end of term. Anna hunched forlornly over a radiator with hers. 'What's wrong?' said Claudia. 'It's going to be fantastic. They're having about forty people. Jack and Ray have got the most amazing collection of records and tapes. Sylvie says they're going to fix up flashing lights.'

'I'll never be allowed to go. Never in a million years. It doesn't end till midnight. And what on earth does "DON'T B.Y.O.B." mean?'

'*Don't Bring Your Own Booze*, idiot,' said Claudia. 'Your mum and dad should like that. They'll think there's not going to be any.'

In the end, Anna decided not to show her invitation at home. She hid it in her coat pocket and got Sylvie to ring up instead, after school had broken up, on the night of the twenty-second. 'It's Sylvie,' she whispered to her mother, cupping a hand over the receiver. 'She says they're having a little party tomorrow, from eight till about ten. Can I go?'

Mrs Hackman nodded. The report Anna had brought home from school had been better than ever. She had just passed her grade five piano examination with distinction. If there couldn't be a little relaxation now, at Christmas time, she didn't know when there ever could be. When Anna replaced the receiver Mrs Hackman remarked how nice it was that Anna had become so friendly with Sylvie. Sylvie must come round and meet Ralph, she said. Maybe Claudia should come too, as Aunt Belle had been so good to Anna. Anna nodded in amazement as she lifted the phone again to arrange a lift for herself to East Edge with one of the other guests. She'd think about getting home after she'd actually arrived. Someone else would be bound to leave early.

The next day, Claudia sat in her room willing the morning away. She was dying to make her escape from Number Nine. Wilf had taken time off from the library for a Christmas break and was always turning up at the door. Not that there had been any word of a wedding. Claudia had never actually succeeded in asking Belle about that, but since her departure there had been no hint of it. At this rate, Claudia thought gloomily, there would be no need for a ceremony. Wilf was treating the place like home anyway – except at night. He still left on the dot of eleven-fifteen. 'Sylvie wants me to go early this afternoon,' she said at lunch time. 'She wants me to be in on all the arrangements. She asked Anna too but Anna reckons she's lucky to be going at all. As it is, she's said she'll be home by ten. I don't know how she thinks she'll manage that. Nobody else'll be leaving.'

'Does Mrs Hackman still make her do all that extra school work?' said Fern. 'Makes me feel guilty. Perhaps I should fix something up for you.'

'Don't bother. The Hackmans are loonies. They'll send Anna round the twist in the end.'

'You could write me some book reviews,' said Wilf. 'I'd really appreciate that and it would be good practice . . .'

Claudia had actually read one of Wilf's books. She had thought herself beyond children's books, but this one had fascinated her. She would have asked Wilf for more by the same author but for her reluctance to indicate that he had in any way got the measure of her. 'Good practice for what?' she retorted, pushing her stool noisily back from the table. As she went upstairs she could hear

Fern apologizing. Minutes later she reappeared with her disco clothes in a carrier bag.

'How're you getting home?' called Fern. 'You can't cycle around at midnight in this sort of weather.'

'I can.'

'Get a lift home. You can go back for your bike in the morning. Promise me you'll get a lift. There're bound to be plenty of parents turning up at midnight.'

Claudia seized her bike and began shoving her way out into the street. 'You're to get a lift,' repeated Fern from the living-room doorway.

'Shut up and get back to your bony boy-friend,' hissed Claudia. 'What's it got to do with you?'

Fern stepped back into the living-room and closed the door. She and Wilf looked at each other, listening to the fight going on in the hall. At last the front door banged and they were on their own. 'She's a real bitch,' quivered Fern. 'I sometimes think I haven't an ounce of feeling left for her.'

Wilf reached out. 'Do you have any for me? That's the point.'

Sylvie's were the first guests to arrive. She had asked ten girls from school. They came in a variety of dress – mini skirts, striped shifts, dungarees, and party dresses chosen by their mothers. They danced together and giggled at comments from Jack and Raymond. 'Those two are getting drunk,' Claudia whispered to Sylvie. 'It'll be all the cider we had earlier.'

'They're used to it,' said Sylvie.

Anna arrived in a brown velvet skirt and waistcoat made by Mrs Hackman from a cut-down dress of her own. Claudia looked her up and down. 'You look really nice in that, Anna. It'd look stupid on me but it really suits you.'

'I could say the same about that thing of yours,' said Anna. 'Is it a nightie?'

Claudia couldn't remember afterwards if she'd been half expecting Raymond to make a beeline for her. Certainly she was surprised by the degree of irritation she felt when he did. She made some attempt to enjoy dancing with him at first, and then excused herself to fetch a drink. 'I'll get it for you' said Raymond. Beads of sweat had formed on his nose. He brushed them away with the back of his hand. 'Don't move.' Anna walked by, arms linked with a schoolmate. 'We've got our eyes on you!' they giggled, waggling their fingers. Raymond came back with a glass of cider. He slid an arm round Claudia's waist while she drank it. 'Let's not dance for a bit,' he whispered. 'We could go outside.'

Claudia stopped drinking and eyed him stonily. 'Get stuffed!' she muttered. She stared round angrily. Across the room Jack was showing off to a throng of girls, not noticing Claudia at all. He needn't think she'd ever want to be a part of his audience, anyway, laughing at his jokes, thinking he was wonderful. She dodged from Ray's grasp and started to dance again on her own – a wild, stomping rampage. Ray's head was the floor beneath her feet. Ray was a *bore* and a *drag* and a *piss-face*.

Sylvie and Anna had joined up in a gang with their school friends. They cavorted to the music and ate a lot of sausages and crisps. 'Anna!' someone called. 'I didn't think drinking was allowed in your family!'

'It isn't,' tittered Anna. 'It's my secret sin. I've had quite a few glasses, actually.'

'Your mum'll smell it, you know. You don't have to be staggering.'

'I can do what I like,' said Anna. In front of everyone she jumped to her feet and skipped tipsily over to Jack. 'Fill me up, Jack.'

Jack led her by the hand to the drinks table and checked through the half-finished cans. 'You're not getting drunk, are you?' he whispered. Anna was swaying slightly against his arm. She was tiny and pretty. Her white cheeks had two high spots of colour. 'I'm not trying to put you down. It can take you by surprise, this stuff.'

'I've had it before,' said Anna. 'We drink like fish in Norfolk. Hasn't Sylvie told you?'

Shortly before ten o'clock, Jack and Raymond decided on a change of mood. They turned off the flashing lights, lit candles instead, and put on a succession of 'slowies'. Raymond pulled

Claudia towards him. Her schoolmates, in a tight bunch, nudged one another and chortled as he lifted her arms round his neck. 'Get off,' she snapped. 'They're all laughing.'

'Ignore them,' murmured Raymond, nuzzling into her shoulder. 'They're just jealous.'

'What of?' hissed Claudia. She shoved at him and suddenly he was falling away, sprawling between people's feet.

'What's going on?' demanded Sylvie, thrusting her face into Claudia's.

'He's drunk,' said Claudia. 'He fell.'

Raymond was scrambling to his feet, rubbing one elbow. 'What did you do that for?'

'You tripped,' said Claudia. 'Someone rammed us.'

Raymond turned to Sylvie, his face red and crumpled. 'She bloody pushed me over.'

They stood in a triangle, glaring at each other, bumped by passing couples. Far away across the room Claudia was aware that the basement door was opening and someone was coming in from outside, stumbling over the threshold, blinking in the half light. It was Wilf Smee. 'Someone for you, Claudia,' a voice was calling.

'I've come for your friend, actually,' Wilf said. 'We've had her mother on the phone half the evening. She's been phoning here and getting no reply. She phoned Fern to see if she'd got the wrong number.'

'Friend? What friend?'

'Anna. Her mother's bothered about lifts back. She couldn't get anyone here to answer the phone.'

'There's nobody in upstairs, that's why.'

'Well, I've come to run her home,' said Wilf. 'Fern's outside. She didn't want you to think she was spying on you so she sent me in. She's scared Anna's going to get in an unholy row at home if she's late.'

They peered round the room for Anna. In the end, Jack switched on the main light and Wilf searched briskly through the pale, shambling groups. Anna was in the cloakroom. She came out ashen and dishevelled. 'Wilf Smee's come for you,' whispered Claudia.

'Aren't you honoured?' Anna seemed dazed. Wilf took her hand and led her quickly away.

Raymond had disappeared also. 'Sick,' said Sylvie. 'He says he bumped his head when he fell but I expect he's drunk. You didn't really push him, did you?'

'I don't think so,' said Claudia.

They sat together in the kitchen, finishing a plate of sausage rolls. 'You could sleep the night,' said Sylvie.

'Your parents won't want guests still hanging around at breakfast. Anyway, I told Mum I'd be back.'

'Nice of her bloke to come for Anna.'

'What was going on between her and Jack?'

'Nothing. She just got him to give her an immense tankard of cider. What was going on between you and Ray? He's gone on you, you know. He made me promise not to say. He had a girl-friend in London once.'

'Just one?'

'Yes. You're the second. Jack's had loads but Ray takes things very seriously. He's sensitive.'

Wilf reappeared at midnight. 'You didn't need to come,' said Claudia, following him up the steps. 'Did Mum send you?' She screwed up her face as she climbed into the car.

'Sorry about the smell,' said Wilf. 'You've got your pal to thank. She was violently sick all the way home.'

Two days later – though it felt more like a week to Claudia, stuck in the house with Wilf and Fern – it was Christmas. For the first time ever Claudia had been actually dreading it. Not that it was usually particularly exciting – Aunt Belle normally came, and took Claudia home with her on Boxing Day – but at least it wasn't unpleasant. This year Belle was staying at Tod's and Wilf Smee was coming instead.

At seven o'clock in the morning, Fern crept into Claudia's room with presents. She seemed excessively eager to please, bearing a cassette recorder and a camera – more lavish gifts than usual, she explained because they were from Wilf too. By eight-thirty, they were down at St Thomas's for their annual Christmas Communion.

And then began the preparations for the meal. Fern seemed especially flustered, cursing as the pudding boiled dry and muttering about a shortage of milk. 'Wilf's not going to care if there's no bread sauce,' said Claudia. 'Not if he's really nuts on you.'

The extent of Fern's agitation continued to be baffling till Claudia opened the front door at half past twelve and confronted Wilf on the doorstep, accompanied by an elderly little woman as skinny as himself. Claudia stared. No wonder Fern had talked her into putting on a skirt. No wonder she'd tarted herself up like a dog's dinner. 'Happy Christmas, Claudia!' Wilf was saying. 'I'd like to introduce my mother.'

Claudia backed down the hallway, muttering 'Happy Christmas!' in return. Then Fern was appearing from behind, a picture of faded gentility in her lace blouse, with wisps of hair escaping from a bun she'd twisted on top of her head. Her skin was creamy but there were pink patches of excitement in her cheeks. Wilf and his mother hopped into the narrow hall like sparrows and introductions began. Claudia watched from half-way up the stairs. Wilf was beaming, adoring Fern as she welcomed his mother.

'I'd've gone out if I'd known she was coming,' Claudia hissed to Fern as she stirred gravy in the kitchen later.

'Don't be ridiculous. You can't foist yourself on friends for Christmas.'

'She has. We don't want her.'

'I do.'

'You could at least have warned me.'

'I knew you'd be like this. At least we had a pleasant morning together. You'd have spoiled that. For my sake, Cloddie, make an effort.'

In the living-room, Wilf poured sherry into the crystal glasses he'd brought as a present for Fern. There had been spare tapes for her recorder for Claudia, and a bottle of French perfume which had delighted her, though no one would have known. 'Sherry, Claudia?'

Mrs Smee's eyebrows rose. 'A bit young, surely,' she murmured.

'Don't be silly, dear,' said Wilf mildly.

'Wilf!' said Fern. 'Your mother's quite right.'

Wilf was handing Claudia her glass. 'Season's greetings, Claudia! Take no notice of that pair.'

He was enjoying linking Fern and his mother in that way, Claudia thought – putting them on the same side, drawing attention to their similar views. 'You and I are in the same boat today,' he was saying. 'Both under the eagle eyes of dear mamas! We'll have to behave.'

Fern and Mrs Smee laughed. Claudia wondered what Mrs Smee was really like behind her pointed little face. She'd planted her feet slightly apart on the Chinese matting, leaving a space between her knees so you could see up to her knickers if you were at the right angle. Fern *was* at the right angle. Claudia sipped at her sherry, grinning broadly to herself. Poor old Fern. She'd be trying not to look up past those knobbly knees. She'd be scared her eyes were somehow going to be drawn, willy-nilly, and then the knees would snap shut suddenly and Mrs Smee would glare and later she'd tell Wilf that Fern wasn't 'nice'. Wilf began to walk round with the sherry bottle again. 'Stop sniggering, Cloddie,' whispered Fern. 'What's the joke?'

Claudia banged her empty glass down on a book-case and ran from the room, stifling her hilarity till she reached the hall. Mrs Smee shifted uneasily. The knees came together. 'Look what you've done, Wilf,' she said. 'It's not a kindness, you know, plying children with alcohol. It's not funny.'

'She giggles all the time,' said Fern. 'It's her age. She doesn't chat on the phone to friends. She just giggles. It's a sort of communal experience.'

Lunch was served in the kitchen. 'Funny without Belle, isn't it?' whispered Claudia as she and Fern put the finishing touches to the table.

'She'll be phoning later. Far better not to make the trip if she's reserving her strength.'

'What do you mean? What's wrong with her?'

'Oh, nothing,' said Fern. Her head was lost in a sudden cloud of steam as she tipped the peas into a colander.

'I want to know. Is she ill or something?'

'Shhh,' said Fern. 'The others'll hear. What are you making

such a fuss about? You've never bothered about Belle before. You needn't start now.'

'Is she ill?'

'No, she's not.'

'Shall we come through?' called Wilf from the other room. 'Do you want a hand?'

Mrs Smee became increasingly interested in Claudia as the meal progressed, making detailed enquiries about school and friends and hobbies. It's because we're sitting opposite each other, Claudia thought. It's because every time we lean forward for a mouthful our heads nearly knock. Later, she began to think it was because Wilf and Fern, mellowing with the food and wine, were becoming rather silent and staring at each other in an embarrassingly moonstruck way. Claudia began to approve of Mrs Smee and the way she kept talking and eating regardless. She herself would have lost her appetite if it hadn't been for Mrs Smee. But, as it was, they both had seconds of everything together and talked non-stop until Fern got up from the table suddenly, followed by Wilf. Their withdrawal, intended to be discreet, put Claudia and Mrs Smee on instant alert. Their chatter died away and their eyes turned sinkwards, where Fern was filling a kettle for coffee. Wilf was taking a small box from his pocket. 'Open it,' he whispered.

'Not now.'

'When?'

'Later.'

'What's going on?' called Mrs Smee, laying down her spoon. 'Don't leave us out.'

Wilf returned to his seat and placed the box in the middle of his table-mat. 'That,' he said, tapping it lightly with a forefinger, 'is a special present to Fern from me. But she's too shy to open it. So I shall just have to sit here till she does.'

'Shhh, Wilf,' said Fern, blinking through strands of hair and spooning coffee into a pot. 'Wait till people have got their coffee.'

'I'm not shy,' said Claudia. 'I'll open it if Mum's being wet.'

Wilf's hand clapped down smartly over the box. 'No, no. It's got to be Fern.'

'You don't need to get jumpy,' muttered Claudia. 'I was only joking.' Suddenly she was prickling with rage. Mrs Smee was silent and staring. 'Come on, Mum. Stop messing about.'

Fern teetered towards the table with the pot and mugs balanced on a tray. Claudia hated her. She'd got them all on toast, waiting and waiting. What the hell was going on? At last Fern picked up the little box and opened it. She held it up close to her face. 'Oh, Wilf, it's beautiful.' Wilf stood up and gazed into the box too. Their heads were touching.

Claudia looked at Mrs Smee again. Her eyes were bright and buttony. 'Aren't you going to show Claudia and me?' she said.

Fern laid the box in the centre of the table. It contained a small silver ring set with a pale stone. Claudia reached out. 'Don't touch,' barked Mrs Smee. 'It's an opal. Bad luck.'

'Don't be ridiculous, Mother,' said Wilf impatiently. 'What an old wives' tale!'

Fern laid a restraining hand on his arm. 'It's lovely. I love it.' She picked up the box, took out the ring and slipped it on the ring finger of her right hand.

'Oh, I see,' said Mrs Smee, briskly pushing her seat back from the table. 'Congratulations are not in order. It's a ring of no particular significance. We were rather excited there for a minute or two, weren't we, Claudia?'

'On the contrary,' said Wilf stiffly. 'It is a ring of very particular significance. Fern's birthday is in October. The opal is her birthstone.'

'Oh, Wilf, how marvellous! I didn't know,' murmured Fern as Mrs Smee went off to the living-room in search of a chair by the fire. She stretched out her fingers and gazed at the stone. 'What a lovely present.'

'Mrs Smee thought it was an engagement ring,' whispered Claudia. 'She nearly had a heart attack.'

Later, Aunt Belle's voice crackled down the line into Claudia's ear. 'Happy Christmas, Cloddie.'

'We've got Wilf and his mum here,' whispered Claudia.

'I've got May Turnbull. We're off to her house now if I can get the car to start. I'm looking forward to you coming, dear.'

'I didn't know I was.'

'I mentioned it to Fern when I was up. If you want to, dear . . .'

'Course I do. It'll be a treat to get away from these two.'

'I've invited Anna. Her mother sent me a nice little card and a note. I rang them up yesterday. It's a wonder Anna didn't say.'

'They've got Ralph home. They're having a little Boxing Day tea tomorrow. Sylvie and I have been invited. I'll see Anna then.'

'Bring Sylvie as well if you'd like to. It was lovely last time. Do come, dear. Give Fern and Wilf a bit of peace to sort things out.'

'Sort what out?'

The living-room door opened. 'Belle?' Fern mouthed. 'Does she want to speak to me?'

Claudia pushed the receiver into her hand and returned to the living-room. She stared balefully from Wilf to his mother and back again. They were talking about Wilf's job. *What you don't realize,* she wanted to shout at Mrs Smee, *is that these two are planning to get married, whatever we think.*

8

A teenagers' tea-party, it was to be, though Anna had done her best to suggest that such a thing was unheard of. In the morning, Mrs Hackman spread doilies on her gold china plates and loaded them with mince pies and slices of Christmas cake. She took her best cups from the cabinet in the dining-room and gave them a dust. 'You'll enjoy this, Anna. You can be mother with the teapot and Ralph can pass round the bits and pieces. You can all chatter away to your hearts' content. It'll be a really civilized little do. I won't interfere at all.'

Anna nodded mutely. Claudia and Sylvie would laugh their heads off. It didn't matter so much for Ralph. He'd invited a couple of lads from his old school because Mrs Hackman had insisted. He wasn't really going to care what they thought. He didn't have friends in Ratfield any more. His friends were scattered all over the globe nowadays, he enjoyed informing people.

The guests had been invited for half-past three. By that time, Mrs Hackman had erected the card-table in the sitting-room and covered it with a lace cloth. There were napkins for everyone and cake-forks and crackers in a fancy box. Anna was wearing her brown velvet again and Ralph his school suit. 'Pinch your cheeks, Anna,' whispered Mrs Hackman as the doorbell rang. 'You look ever so peaky. People will think there's been a death.'

It was Claudia. She'd come on her bike and stood on the doorstep apple-cheeked, her curls in tight black knots all over her head. 'Happy Christmas, Mrs Hackman!'

'Thank you,' said Mrs Hackman, straightening her Paisley pattern dress. 'And the same to you, dear. We don't seem to have seen so much of you recently. The days just seem to fly past.'

As Claudia took her coat off in the hall, the dining-room door opened and Mr Hackman, in his shirt-sleeves and laden with books, darted out and sped towards the stairs. 'Don't mind Anna's dad,' whispered Mrs Hackman. 'He doesn't have holidays like the rest of us.' She ushered Claudia towards the sitting-room. 'I'm just the butler today,' she said, wrinkling up her nose to show it was a joke. 'I'm not allowed into the party.'

Claudia walked on alone into the sitting-room. 'My God!' she gasped, clapping a hand over her mouth. 'What's all this?'

'Mum's idea,' mumbled Anna.

Claudia dropped on to the sofa with a bounce and crossed her legs. 'Looks very nice,' she said. 'Are you going to offer me something, Ralph?'

Ralph was leaning stiffly against the mantelpiece. He resented Claudia's cockiness. He always had. As far as he could see, she had precious little to be cocky about. 'Not till everyone's arrived.'

'Oh, I see. Putting me in my place. Not very gentlemanly.'

'You can't be much of a lady or you wouldn't have asked.'

'For goodness' sake!' said Anna. 'Can't you two even try to get on? Give her something, Ralph!'

'Who else is coming?' asked Claudia.

'Hardly anyone,' said Anna.

By the time the others arrived, Claudia had managed to overcome the temptation to spend the afternoon baiting Ralph. For Anna's sake she wanted the party to be a success, and to some extent, she felt, Ralph couldn't be blamed for being objectionable. He hadn't asked to be sent to a snob school. He might have been perfectly all right if his parents hadn't decided to have him trained up as something he wasn't. She beamed broadly as Sylvie came in, followed by two shuffling boys, purple to the ears. 'Wotcha, mate,' one of them muttered gruffly to Ralph. 'How's tricks?' Ralph turned away in confusion and seized one of his mother's plates of mince pies.

Almost before the first blushes of discomfort had faded from anybody's cheeks, there was a coy tap at the door. 'Kettle's boiling, Anna,' called Mrs Hackman. 'Don't worry, anyone. I'm not coming in.'

'It looks a delicious tea, Mrs Hackman,' Sylvie called back.

'Greaser!' said Claudia.

The two boys laughed but Ralph remained silent. In fact, the next hour passed very agreeably with almost no comment from Ralph at all. The other boys knew Sylvie's brothers at school and told ribald stories about them to make the girls giggle. They didn't actually want to leave Ralph out, but having had the luck to hit on an area of ground common to five of the people present, they were reluctant to shift from it. Towards the end of the afternoon, as Anna handed round more cups of tea, Ralph circulated the box of crackers. They were red and shiny and went off with a good series of bangs, leaving everyone jumpy and excited. Claudia's contained an indoor firework which fizzled ineffectually on a saucer for two or three minutes, making a disgusting smell. 'I think I'd better clear that away,' said Anna. 'I don't think we should have lit it really. Mum'll have a fit if it's stained her saucer.' She jumped up anxiously as Ralph reached over her head with a cup of tea for Sylvie. For a split second Claudia had a distinct impression of its flight through the air – a pale blue comet, trailing a tail of brown tea – before it crashed into the wall above the fireplace.

Mrs Hackman was through the door before anyone had time to move. 'You're so hopeless, Anna,' she wailed. 'You can't even manage a cup of tea, can you? That's an heirloom you've smashed . . . would've been yours one day . . . you've destroyed it already . . . got yourself to thank . . .'

Claudia stood up quietly and went over to the fireplace. 'I did it, Mrs Hackman,' she said, kneeling to pick up the pieces. 'I'm terribly sorry.' Mrs Hackman gaped down at the top of the curly head. 'I'm not used to bone china,' said Claudia. She stood up and examined the pieces in her hand. 'It won't stick, will it?'

'Of course it won't stick!' snapped Mrs Hackman. 'It's ruined. But don't apologize to me. It's Anna's. Apologize to her.' She hurried off to fetch a bucket and cloth. She was still on her knees, scrubbing the edge of the carpet and dabbing at the wall, when everyone left half an hour later.

'Thank you,' Anna whispered to Claudia in the hall.

Claudia shrugged. 'She doesn't like me anyway. She'll be kicking herself for ever thinking I could be trusted with a teacup.'

Ralph wheeled a trolley out of the sitting-room. He stopped and eyed Claudia coldly. 'You didn't need to martyr yourself. We can cope with our own mother, you know.' He turned to Anna. 'I know her sort. Don't kid yourself. She's sneering at us. She thinks we're pathetic.'

Aunt Belle had said she would wait for them in Cranwick again. They spotted her from the bus, huddled on a bench, head sunk in her fur collar. They peered at her curiously as the bus drew up. She was motionless but for her hair, tossed in all directions by the stiff breeze. 'What's wrong with her?' whispered Anna.

'Nothing,' said Claudia. 'Get your stuff.'

On the pavement, people milled around them, running for buses, dragging heavy luggage towards the waiting-room. The wind was icy. 'It's colder than Ratfield,' grumbled Sylvie.

Claudia stopped. 'You two wait here. I think she's asleep. She'll feel a fool if we all spring up on her.'

Sylvie and Anna, teeth chattering, watched as Claudia ran ahead. She tapped the fur coat lightly and Aunt Belle gave a little jump. Then she was on her feet, hurrying towards them with her lopsided gait. 'Hibernating!' she said. 'Dress like a squirrel, act like a squirrel!'

'We'll have to buy you a bag of nuts,' said Anna. She gave Aunt Belle a kiss.

Sylvie grinned. 'I've got a cold,' she said. 'Don't come near me.'

Claudia watched the others greeting Aunt Belle and getting excited as their journey neared its end. There was a tight feeling in her chest. Something was wrong with Aunt Belle. It didn't matter what anybody said, or how vehemently they denied it . . . When she'd nudged Aunt Belle like that, it had been like bringing her back to life. She'd been so utterly still, like a heart that had stopped beating – till Claudia had got her going again. And how long would she keep on going?

The kitchen was full of good smells. They sat straight down at the table and Belle served Irish stew with dumplings, and a little red wine. 'I want to propose a toast,' she said. 'Don't drink for a minute.' Outside, the sky was heavy and dark. She lit a candle and set it in the middle of the table and they all lifted their glasses. 'To your next visit,' said Belle. 'And your next and your next.'

'To our next visit,' they chanted. 'And our next and our next.'

'We haven't started this one yet,' said Anna.

It was to be a shorter stay than last time, as Mrs Hackman insisted on having Anna back in plenty of time to prepare for school the following Monday. Most days were cold and wet. Sleet beat against the windows and lowering skies made the rooms dark. Sylvie and Claudia stayed inside, drinking mugs of cocoa round the Aga, while Belle and Anna made expeditions into the village in the car. One day they were gone for four hours. Claudia added water to soup that was boiling dry on the stove and sat at the table fidgeting with the cutlery they had set for lunch.

'Nothing will have happened,' said Sylvie. 'Stop worrying. You've been edgy about Aunt Belle ever since we got here. What's wrong?'

'I think she's ill. Remember how we found her? Unconscious, practically. That wasn't like her at all. She's a bustling sort of person.'

'She was dozing. She'd just dropped off with the boredom of waiting.'

'She *is* ill. I'm sure she is.'

Sylvie examined her reflection in the back of a spoon. 'Don't be mad if I say something . . .'

'What?'

'I've sometimes wondered if she's got a drink problem – d'you know what I mean? She drinks like a whale. Glass after glass. I've seen little half-finished glasses all over the house. I think she's having little secret nips of this and that all the time.'

'Oh, you've seen them. So've I. I brought a couple down from upstairs and started washing them up one day, but she got quite snappy and told me to leave the glasses to her in future. She never seems drunk, though, does she? Not like the winos down our street. They don't seem to know what's going on half the time.'

'No, she's never drunk. Though with that limp of hers you can't really tell if she's staggering or not.'

Claudia began to giggle. 'Poor old thing – written off as a drunk when she's just a harmless cripple!'

'Don't laugh like that, Cloddie.'

Claudia crammed a hanky over her mouth. Her shoulders shook and tears streamed down her cheeks. 'I'm not really laughing,' she gasped. 'I've been thinking all week that she's dying. I haven't been able to get it out of my head.'

'Whatever you do, Cloddie, don't say that sort of thing to Anna.'

'What's Anna got to do with it?'

'She dotes on Aunt Belle. You know that. They've been writing letters ever since last time. Aunt Belle and Mrs Hackman are really matey. Anna told me.'

'Nobody could be matey with Mrs Hackman. Aunt Belle just went round there to be polite – so Mrs Hackman could see what she was like. She went round to see your mum too.'

'Yes, but that was all very businesslike. She just more or less thanked Mum for letting me come here as company for you. And Mum thanked her for having me. It was different at the Hackmans'. They had a real heart-to-heart, Anna says.'

Claudia blew her nose sharply. 'I'm sick of Anna, if you want to know. First Aunt Belle thinks she's marvellous and now here's you, telling me to keep my trap shut in case the poor little thing gets upset. What about me? I'm upset. It's my bloody aunt.'

A car horn sounded outside. 'It's them!' said Sylvie. She caught Claudia's arm. 'I'm sorry, Cloddie,' she said. 'I didn't think you were all that attached to her. You've always moaned about how deadly it used to be coming here on your own. And Anna's such a weakling. You're so strong . . .'

'That's what they all say,' said Claudia. 'The weaklings get the best of it, though, don't they?'

The door opened and Anna stood there, dripping and gabbling. They had been at May Turnbull's – an old friend of Belle's. There'd been a flood in her house. They'd been mopping up for hours. 'Belle's going back this afternoon. She's a poor old woman all on her own. Belle's going to see to it all.'

Claudia managed only one evening talk alone with Belle. Though she invented nightly pretexts for sneaking downstairs after the others were in bed, it was only on the last night that she actually found Belle still in the kitchen. She was leaning against the sink, waiting for the kettle to boil and singing to herself. They had all been playing charades by candlelight. The candles were guttering in hot pools of wax. 'Hullo, Cloddie!'

Claudia came in hesitantly and slid into a chair at the kitchen table. 'Can we talk a bit? I've been coming down all week but I've always missed you.'

'Worn out by you three,' said Belle with a wink.

'You aren't ill, are you?'

Belle turned off the kettle and began pouring hot water into a rubber hot-water bottle. 'Just old age, dear.'

'You're not very old.'

'Not ancient, I suppose.' Belle sat down, the hot-water bottle on her lap, and studied Claudia's lowered head. 'What's all this about? Ten minutes to get it off your chest, then up you go.'

'I've felt so worried,' mumbled Claudia, drawing patterns on the table-top with her finger. 'Since before Christmas I've had this idea you were ill. I can't get rid of it. You'd tell me, wouldn't you, if there was anything wrong?'

'Is that really all that's bothering you?' said Belle. 'It isn't anything else? Like Fern and Wilf, say, for instance . . .?'

'I'm not the least bit bothered about them. Should I be? What's there to bother about?'

'If they were to get married . . .' Claudia's heart thumped. Aunt Belle saying it like that! Without turning a hair! '. . . You mustn't think you wouldn't be wanted. Fern would never part with you.'

'There's times I wouldn't mind parting with her,' muttered Claudia. 'If they really did get married I'd rather live with you. That's what I'd really like to do. Boozy holidays all the time. Great!'

'Cloddie . . .'

'Friends to stay whenever I felt like it. Nobody being snooty about where I live or who my parents are, or aren't.'

'Cloddie . . .'

'Aren't you lonely on your own, Aunt Belle? Isn't that why you like having us to stay? Wouldn't you like me to be permanent?'

'Cloddie . . . That's not the point, is it? I don't come into this. The important thing is for you and Fern to stick together. It'll count for something if you can look each other in the eye in ten years' time, knowing you never let each other down.'

'I was only joking,' said Claudia stonily. 'They won't marry, anyway. There's no chance.'

'Do try to accept Wilf a bit, dear. It'd make life so much easier for Fern . . .'

'And we all want an easy life for Fern.'

'. . . She's very fond of him. But you're probably right, she won't marry him if you're against it.'

'Well, that's not love, is it? Poor old Wilf if he's got to hang around waiting for my seal of approval.' Claudia chuckled. Aunt Belle sighed so deeply that for a moment Claudia thought she was yawning. 'I'll go up, Aunt Belle. You're exhausted.'

'The point is, she loves both of you,' said Belle. 'Different kinds of love . . . They don't need to conflict. It would help so much if you could try and see that.'

'Of course I can see it,' said Claudia. 'She'd need to be deranged to love a full-grown man in the way she loves me! If you can call Wilf full-grown, that is.'

'Different kinds of love,' murmured Belle. 'But not incompatible. That's what you need to understand. You feel threatened, Cloddie. That's why you've concocted the fantasy of living with me.'

Claudia stood up. 'I wasn't serious. I told you that. Just as well, as you've made it perfectly clear I wouldn't be welcome. God knows why you have me to stay as often as you do. Oh yes, the easy life for Fern – anyway, you prefer me diluted these days, it seems. Anna's the one you really want to see.'

One of the candles went out suddenly, leaving the room surprisingly darker. Claudia glanced at Belle, wondering why she didn't reply. 'Aunt Belle! Don't cry! I don't mean the things I say. They just pop out.'

'It's not that,' whispered Belle. 'I just feel tired and feeble. I thought I could do so much for you and Fern. But I can't. I can't do a thing.' She sat motionless, staring at her hands resting on the hot-water bottle in her lap.

Claudia shoved her stool back. She dropped on her knees beside

Belle's chair. 'You do everything for Mum and me. You always have. Just having you here at Tod's makes all the difference to us. I'm sorry I've always been a monster.' She took one of Belle's hands and kissed it.

Upstairs, Sylvie and Anna had fallen asleep with the light on. Claudia switched it off and crept into her own bed. She lay for a long time squirming at the memory of her spasm of affection downstairs. Kissing Belle's hand, for God's sake! But she had wanted to.

9

'Would you describe my mother as a "loose" woman?' asked Claudia. 'You're a bookish sort of bloke. How would you describe her?'

Wilf looked up from his newspaper. They were both in the living-room waiting for Fern. They had been conjecturing reasons for her delay. It was a fortnight since Claudia and the others had returned from Tod Pool to start the new term. Wilf gazed steadily at Claudia for a moment, then stretched out his legs in turn to adjust his socks.

Twit! thought Claudia. Blink-blinking his beady little eyes, twitching at his little woolly socks. She could just picture him at work – books in his briefcase, books under his arms, books all over his desk. He'd be forever examining them for damage, stamping their fronts, lining them up on shelves. Someone like Wilf was enough to put you off reading for life.

'I've brought you some more books,' said Wilf. 'I gather you rather liked the last lot. I've got a bit of a mixed bag here. You're a challenging age to cater for, you know.' He began to pull books from his case – two by the author Claudia had secretly liked earlier, one that looked historical, *Wuthering Heights*, and *Rebecca*.

'How did you know I liked any of the last lot?' said Claudia.

'Fern said she saw you reading one of them about three times.'

'She's so nosy. She spies on me all the time. She'd be the same with you, you know.'

'With me . . .?'

'If you got hitched. She'd be into your business all the time. You wouldn't have a life to call your own.'

'Oh, I see. You're thinking in terms of our getting hitched.'

'Not me. Aunt Belle.'

Wilf stood up and walked to the window. He didn't want to

continue with this if Fern was in sight. 'What did you think of the idea?'

'Idea?'

'Of Fern and me marrying.'

Claudia's tongue seemed to be swelling up. It filled her mouth so there was hardly room to make words. 'Nothing. I didn't think anything of the idea. I thought she was going ga-ga to suggest it. Fern's not at all your type. Or your mother's. She's 'loose', I think you'd probably say. 'Fast and loose'. I was asking you just now. I didn't spring from behind a gooseberry bush, you know.'

'I imagine not,' said Wilf, sitting down again. 'Though, if you don't mind my saying so, you're sufficiently prickly to have had that sort of progeniture.' He laughed self-consciously and crossed his arms and legs. 'I knew we'd have to have this kind of talk some time.'

'Oh?' Claudia raised her eyebrows. 'What kind of talk? I wasn't aware we were having any particular kind. I thought this was general chit-chat, filling in till Mum comes in with the supper.'

'I do want to marry your mother,' said Wilf. 'I seem to remember telling you that before. I want . . .'

Claudia was speaking before his sentence was finished. 'Of course you do. Why shouldn't you? You're not the first. Nor the last, I don't suppose. There's been men in and out of here ever since I can remember. The only one I don't think I ever set eyes on at all was my father. He was just in and out the once, I think. You do know all about me, don't you? I'm not a kid sister of Fern's or anything like that. I'm her daughter. I was conceived in the normal way. That should tell you a lot about her. But not much about me – not that you'd be interested. I don't actually like this 'kind of talk', as you put it. I don't feel I know you well enough to be discussing your designs on my mother. Speak to *her* about it, for God's sake. It's got nothing to do with me.'

When Fern came home, Wilf was alone in the living-room. 'She's upstairs,' he sighed. 'We'll have to cool it for a week or two. She bolted. I imagine I've set everything back by about ten years.'

*

84

'Why don't you ask your mother straight out?' Sylvie said. It was dinner time, and wet. She and Anna were standing round a radiator with Claudia in the school hall.

'She won't actually marry him,' said Anna. 'There's no room in your house for anyone else.'

'We could move, stupid,' said Claudia. 'Anyway, he wouldn't take up much space, would he? He'd be sharing her bedroom, after all.'

'Flipping heck!' snorted Sylvie. 'You'd really hear them at it then!'

'I've heard them already, don't you worry.'

'No, you haven't,' said Anna. 'That was just imagination. Your mother's not like that.'

'Not like that! Course she's like that. How do you think I got here? She's like that all right.'

'Calm down,' said Sylvie. 'Everyone's like that. How do you think any of us got here? Your mum's no different from anyone else.'

'I hate her. She could have had me adopted, couldn't she? I could have landed up somewhere really good. But she had to keep me, didn't she? She had to make sure I ended up on the same muck-heap as her. *Bitch*!'

Sylvie ran her hands uneasily along the ridged top of the radiator. This wasn't the first time Claudia had ended up cursing her mother.

'You scare me when you go on like that, Cloddie,' whispered Anna.

Claudia whipped round to face her. 'Scare you, do I? Is that all the bloody help you're going to be? Is that it – your great contribution?' She spun on her heel. From a distance of ten yards she called, 'I'm so sorry. You're such a sensitive, pampered little pair. I shouldn't have troubled you with my sordid problems.'

Not for the first time, Sylvie and Anna were left gaping at each other, sharing the same mixed feelings. Claudia's dilemma was miserable but it didn't give her the right to take it out on them. She ought to be grateful for their sympathy. Instead she was storming off, leaving them feeling inadequate – as if, when it came to the crunch, they were no earthly use to anyone. 'It's just me she's mad with,' said Anna. 'Go after her if you want.'

'She's mad with everyone.'

'We'd be like that in her place.'

Sylvie nodded, ashamed of the intensity of her relief at being in no such place. She was sure Anna felt the same. Perhaps that was why Claudia had turned her back on them – spurning the consolation of friends who, deep down, were so thankful not to be her or to share any of her problems.

Over the next fortnight, Claudia's panic subsided. Wilf's visits to Number Nine became less frequent and there seemed, after all, nothing to panic about. On the rare occasions when she found herself alone with him, she talked politely about books. Wilf jotted down her opinions of new authors in a notebook – to pass on to his children's librarian, he said. Claudia felt flattered. She picked up her friendships with Anna and Sylvie as casually as if she had never flung them aside. 'As far as I can make out I'm practically running the children's section of Wilf's library!' she told them.

'You might get to like him in the end,' said Anna. 'That would be nice.'

'*Never*! He's a nit! Imagine running to his little assistant and telling her to order this and that because *I* said so!'

Anna and Sylvie exchanged smiles. Putting up with the vagaries and violence of Claudia's moods was the least they could do to improve her lot, they'd agreed. They were pleased to have her wit and vigour in their midst again. Unknown to Claudia, they were now meeting regularly outside school and building up a trouble-free, if unchallenging, friendship without her. Mrs Hackman was pleased. In her opinion, involvement with the Lamonts was infinitely preferable to being entangled in the dubious goings-on at Candlemaker Row.

Fern put down the phone and trudged upstairs. In her bedroom, Claudia was writing a composition about the sort of house she'd most like to own one day. Rather to her surprise, hers was beginning to sound a bit like Tod Pool. Wilf was coming round later. She'd show him the composition and see what he thought of

86

it. Recently he'd read an old one which had been lying around and he'd been very impressed.

'Am I disturbing you?' said Fern.

'Of course. What d'you want?'

'That was Belle on the phone, checking if you wanted to go to Tod's at Easter. She says take Anna and Sylvie again if you like.'

'I suppose I'll have to – go, and take them. You'll be running off to one of your courses. And Anna will have a fit if she's left behind.'

'Did Belle seem all right when you were there last time? It didn't seem too much for her, did it?'

'No. She spent half the time seeing to an old woman with a burst pipe.'

'She seemed OK, then?'

'*Yes*. Isn't she OK? We've had all this before. Is she ill or isn't she?'

'She's getting older. Use your sense. Old people shouldn't overdo things.'

Claudia's chest was in the grip of a vice suddenly. 'I *know* she's ill, whatever you say. – And I know you're going to marry Wilf Smee.'

Fern blushed deeply. 'What on earth is the connection between Belle's health and Wilf and me?' she asked, with a little laugh.

'She seemed to think you might marry Wilf. Will you?'

Fern shook her head lightly. 'I shouldn't think so for a minute. I wonder what gave her that impression. She certainly shouldn't have mentioned it to you. Wilf hasn't even asked me.'

'That's a lie,' said Claudia, throwing down her pen. 'That's another of your damn lies. I hope you're straighter with him than you are with me. I hope you've told him properly about me, for instance. And he knows about all the other men you've had, apart from him and my father, does he? You'll have to tell him, you know. And his mother. She'll have to know what's joining the family.'

'Shut up, Cloddie,' snapped Fern. 'You don't upset me any more. In fact, you're turning into a real bore. Wilf and his mother have a perfectly accurate notion of what I'm like. I've had no lovers, as you know perfectly well. Just a few friends. This 'slut' and 'tart' business is all a fabrication of yours.'

'Not quite,' said Claudia. 'Else how do you account for me?'

For weeks, Raymond Lamont had been secretly longing to make new approaches to Claudia. He had composed numerous letters to her in his head, as well as committing some to paper, suggesting a variety of meetings and outings, any of which might have been feasible had he not always lost his nerve at the last minute and failed to post anything through her letter-box. However, towards the end of term, the Sports Centre was having a fund-raising disco and, at last, he plucked up his courage. Claudia found a pale green envelope just inside the front door when she arrived home from school. She read it disdainfully. Raymond flipping Lamont! Why not Jack or even supercilious Ralph? She shoved the letter behind a candlestick on the mantelpiece and later showed it to Fern. 'We really manage to pick up the dregs, don't we?'

The same evening, Sylvie phoned to say that she was going to the disco with a friend of Jack's and Jack had invited Anna. So they'd all be going.

'Jack's invited *Anna*!'

'Mmm. He says she's very beautiful. I sent him round to do it in person. He made a great impression on Mrs Hackman.'

'I thought Jack had millions of girl-friends.'

'He has. But he never likes anything to get serious. He hardly ever asks anyone out. He just meets up with people. He's only asking Anna because she's a friend of mine.' She lowered her voice. 'It's Ray who's serious. He's upstairs jittering like a cat in a cage, wanting to know if you're coming or not.'

'What d'you mean, "serious"?'

'He really likes you. I told you he did. He always goes bright red if I mention you. You must come.'

As soon as Claudia replaced the receiver it rang again. It was Anna. 'It's me, Cloddie. Mum says I can have two minutes. Jack Lamont's asked me to a disco. He says you're going with Raymond. What are you going to wear? Do you think my brown will do?'

'I suppose so. Jack's seen you in it before. It doesn't seem to have put him off.'

'He doesn't fancy me or anything. He told Mum that he and Raymond were asking Sylvie's friends just for the fun of it. Mum thought it sounded rather nice.'

'Do you think it really is just that? Sylvie says Ray likes me. I don't want him all over me again like at their party. I don't want to start anything.'

'Oh, I think he's quite shy, Cloddie. I don't think he'll do anything you don't want. There'll be no drink this time, remember. You are going, aren't you, Cloddie?'

Some nights later, Raymond turned up at the door of Number Nine with a daffodil stuck in the front of his sweater and reeking, as Fern observed to Wilf on her return to the living-room, like a brewery. 'I haven't been able to eat a bite all day,' he told Claudia, taking her arm along the pavement. 'One of the lads gave me a couple of cans or I don't think I'd have dared come.' At the end of the street he perched on the side of a concrete litter bin, his hair blown up in a cock's comb by passing buses. 'I'm really gone on you,' he shouted. 'Now I'm paralytic I don't care what I say.'

At the Centre, the others were waiting. They cheered as Raymond and Claudia approached hand in hand. 'He says he's pissed out of his mind,' muttered Claudia to Sylvie. 'He refused to come unless I held his hand.'

Mr Tetworth, on the door, took their tickets. He patted Raymond's pockets and held him back while the others went through. 'Checking he's not bringing cans in,' muttered Jack. 'Stupid idiot. Where did he get it? Tet's dead strict.'

'He said a friend gave him a couple of cans,' said Claudia. 'He said he wouldn't have dared come for me otherwise.'

Jack cast her a withering sideways glance. 'Something special about you, is there?' He turned away and helped Anna off with her coat. Sylvie and her partner were already gyrating under the spinning lights.

'Got away with it!' Raymond's glistening, pustular face thrust itself into Claudia's. He led her on to the floor, adjusting his daffodil and hailing friends loudly. Claudia danced in circles, trying to blot out the sight of him. At refreshment time he leaned on her shoulder, mumbling that this had to be the best night of his life. Claudia was silent. She could smell his cheese and onion crisps. People had started to dance again. They looked half mad, eyes and teeth flashing. She glared at Anna and Sylvie, dancing the night away, abandoning her to this dolt . . . When Raymond excused himself abruptly to go to 'the bog', she moved swiftly from the small area they'd occupied all evening and found herself another partner in another part of the hall.

'Do they all drink like that?' asked Fern. 'Wilf and I were worried all evening.'

'Ray's an idiot. He's just trying to act big. There's lots like him at Ratfield Boys'. They drink and act stupid. They usually throw up all over the place in the end. We've had a woman in at school talking about drink.'

'How old is he?' said Wilf. 'Sixteen or something? I've never heard the like.'

'Stick around, Wilfie-boy!' said Claudia. 'You ain't seen nuttin' yet!'

Wilf threw back his head and guffawed. 'He thinks we're being all jokey together,' Claudia thought. 'He thinks I'm on his side.'

10

Fern and Wilf decided to drive the girls to Belle's for their Easter visit. Claudia, who considered the bus journeys there and back an integral part of a Tod Pool visit, felt cheated, but Anna and Sylvie relished the prospect of vetting Wilf and forming first-hand impressions of his relationship with Fern.

'No nudging or giggling in the car,' said Sylvie. 'We'll compare notes in bed the first night.'

'I've told you about them already,' said Claudia. 'You know what they're up to.'

'We only know what you think. We'll pretend they're complete strangers and see how they strike us.'

Wilf called for Sylvie first, and then stopped off at Winchester Road for Anna. Mrs Hackman kept him talking in the hall while her husband loaded luggage into the back of Wilf's red estate car. Afterwards she declared Wilf to be absolutely charming. It must be some regrettable aberration on his part if Aunt Belle was right in supposing him to be seriously enamoured of Fern Spark.

'She looks a perfectly nice woman,' said Mr Hackman. 'Not easy, bringing up a child single-handed.'

'No,' said Mrs Hackman. 'And if she'd behaved herself in the first place she wouldn't have needed to. She's always running round with her clothes hanging off her and holes in her tights. And Claudia fills Anna's head with the most hair-raising tales.'

'Vivid imagination, that's all. Probably needs a firm hand.'

'Well, I'm certain Mr Smee has no idea what he's getting into,' said Mrs Hackman. She opened a cupboard and took out cleaning things. Ralph was expected home with a friend – the son of someone in the Foreign Office. 'Still, thank goodness we've got Anna's bedroom free. Ralph's guest won't be used to sharing.'

Mr Hackman stretched out his felt-slippered feet and chuckled.

'Not at home, maybe. But they get no privacy at school. Think of those dormitories.'

Mrs Hackman smiled too. Anna's report had been excellent again. Mr Hackman had been promoted to head of department, and now Ralph was bringing home a distinguished guest. 'I'm going to ease up on my pills, Frank. I'm going to see Dr Sylvester about it.'

At Candlemaker Row, Fern and Claudia were waiting on the doorstep. 'Why are you and Wilf driving us down this time?' asked Claudia. 'What's the real reason? Not like you to give up one of your courses.'

'Wilf doesn't know Norfolk at all. He needs a break. We'll have a couple of days along the coast.'

'We like the bus.'

'Mrs Hackman wasn't exactly heartbroken to be told she could save the fare. We're not going to stay at Belle's, you know. Only long enough to give Wilf a glimpse of Tod's. We're not going to get in your way.'

The car arrived with Anna and Sylvie in the back, silently scrutinizing Wilf's crinkly head. Claudia squeezed in between them. 'Hi!'

'Shhh. We don't want to miss this bit.'

Wilf had got out of the car. He was greeting Fern with the slightest of kisses and bending to pick up a case. 'That's just because you're gaping at him,' said Claudia. 'You're cramping his style.'

It was a long and silent journey. The car sped down motorways for two hours, threading in and out of lanes, slowing slightly at road works, with scarcely a word exchanged by its occupants. 'It's us!' Fern whispered to Wilf as she bent to adjust the radio. 'They're intrigued out of their minds. Heaven knows what Cloddie's told them!' As soon as they left the motorway, Wilf stopped at a roadside café and they sat under an umbrella, drinking coffee and Coke. 'What do you do while you're at Tod Pool?' Wilf asked Anna. 'What's the great attraction?'

'Just being with Aunt Belle, really. She's such a nice person. I play lots of music with her. She's got stacks of duets from when she was a girl. She says she's reliving her past with me.'

'How about you, Sylvie?'

'I like going off to the beach best – just the three of us.'

'It's very nice for Claudia that you both like Tod's so much,' said Fern. 'I think she was a bit lonely at Belle's sometimes, weren't you, Cloddie?'

'Anybody would be – knowing they'd just been packed off for convenience. It didn't stop you sending me.'

'I wouldn't mind being packed off to Tod's every day of the week,' said Sylvie.

Claudia sucked at her straw. Sylvie was a big idiot – all freckly and grinning. She didn't know what she was talking about. She hadn't a clue what it was like having Fern for a mother and no father at all. There wasn't a complete stranger muscling his way into her family, shoving her over to make room for himself. There wasn't a voice constantly nagging in the back of her head, *They wish you weren't here . . . you're in the way . . .*

From the very start, the visit went badly. Fern and Wilf didn't leave straight away. Belle insisted on giving them tea in the sitting-room while the girls had theirs in the kitchen. After that, she almost succeeded in persuading them to stay the night, and when they refused and eventually did leave she slumped miserably in an armchair with a huge whisky. 'She seems to want them more than us,' whispered Anna. It was only with very obvious effort that Belle pulled herself together and sent the girls off for a brisk cliff-top walk while she prepared supper.

Claudia came running home ahead of the others. She stopped suddenly in the back yard instead of bursting in through the kitchen door and crept up to one of the steamy windows. Aunt Belle was prodding something in a pan. Whatever it was was proceeding satisfactorily and Belle replaced the pan lid and reached out for her glass. She sipped from it, set it down and then, all of a sudden, her knees seemed to buckle. She clutched at one of the wooden chairs and collapsed on to it, throwing her arms and head forward over the table. Claudia froze. Behind her she could hear Anna and Sylvie turning in at the gate. She moved away from the window. 'Beat you!' she called loudly. 'I've been waiting ages.' She jostled them when they caught up with her, delaying their entry to the kitchen by several minutes. When they did troop in together, nobody was there.

The consensus of opinion at bedtime was that Fern and Wilf were just pegging along as friends. They hadn't given the impression of being madly sexually attracted to each other, nor even passionately devoted in a less physical way. Claudia could stop worrying about an imminent marriage. There probably would never be one. 'I think he's rather nice,' said Sylvie. 'Actually, he seemed more interested in us than her. I think he really enjoyed talking to us at the café.'

'He's too bony. He's like a skeleton. I don't know how Mum can bring herself to touch him.'

'She probably doesn't,' said Anna. 'People aren't nearly as keen on that as you'd think. I've seen it in the papers.'

Sylvie snorted. 'Course they're keen on it.'

'Well, I'm nearly fourteen and nothing's ever happened to me. Nor to you either, I bet. Or Cloddie.'

'I've been kissed,' said Claudia flatly. 'If that's what you're on about.'

'Who hasn't?' said Sylvie. 'In London we used to be friendly with another family and while the parents sat in the sitting-room having sherry and stuff we used to go upstairs and play kissing games.'

'You never told me you'd been kissed, Cloddie,' said Anna suspiciously. 'Was it Raymond?'

'I don't tell you everything. No, it wasn't Raymond. I've been kissed dozens of times after discos. It's no great deal.' Claudia turned over and closed her eyes. In the dark Anna and Sylvie were whispering. It was like the first time they'd come.

'Don't ask about Ray,' Sylvie was saying. 'She was really horrible to him. He's had a complex about being repulsive ever since that disco. I'd be really cross if it was anyone else. But Mum says you've got to make allowances for someone like Claudia. Well, we've been doing that for ages, really, haven't we? She's bound to have problems – with her set-up.'

It was Anna who first actually put it into words as they sat on the churchyard wall in the sunshine, surveying thick clumps of daffodils. 'Aunt Belle's changed, hasn't she? Do you think she's depressed? She's weepy – like Mum used to be.'

'Weepy?' said Claudia.

'Yesterday afternoon when we were playing duets. She said it was the music.'

'Perhaps it was,' said Sylvie. 'People do cry over music.'

'I know all that,' said Anna. 'She just seems different, that's all.'

They swung their legs and shared out a bar of chocolate. 'I must say,' said Sylvie, 'she's hitting the bottle a bit. And she's not really bothering with us much, is she? Not like before.'

Claudia jumped off the wall suddenly and brushed the crumbs from her jeans. 'I can't stand it. I thought you two hadn't noticed. I'm going to ask her.'

That evening, they fished for whiting from the boat belonging to Dr Hainge from Wet Sands. His student grandson, Matthew, skippered, heading the boat out across the still waters of the harbour towards the open sea. Aunt Belle sat beside Claudia, instructing the girls on the use of the lines, and baiting the hooks with mussels. 'It's just like the old days,' she said. 'I used to come in this very boat with my brother and Matthew's grandfather. We anchored just beyond the headland, above the wreckage of an old boat that went down years ago.' Matthew nodded and said he was heading for the same spot. The fishing there was still the best. As they began to feel the swell of the waves, Belle handed out the wooden frames wrapped round with thick line. 'Wait till we anchor,' she called above the gathering wind, 'and keep your frames in the bottom of the boat. Hold them down with your feet. We don't want to lose anything overboard.' Claudia's spirits soared. Belle's eyes were shining. Her cheeks streamed with the spray that flew in over the side.

By the time Matthew headed back to shore, seventeen whiting lay in a heap at their feet, silver-bellied and gleaming. Claudia jumped as one twitched against her foot. Its jaws gaped slowly. 'It's sad they're dying,' she said.

Belle nodded. They were entering calm waters again. Above and around them, sea and sky were steely, streaked with the last vestiges of light. Ahead, the land was black. 'Wait till they're sizzling in a pan. They aren't tiddlers. They've had their day.'

Matthew helped them ashore – Belle first, carrying the fish in a string bag. Claudia was last. 'Thank you,' she said. 'I think my aunt enjoyed it more than anybody!'

'She looks fine,' he agreed. 'You'd never guess . . .'

Claudia stumbled to the end of the quay. 'You look drunk,' shouted Anna. 'Isn't it queer? I'm still going up and down. Are you?'

'Come up to the car,' whispered Claudia. 'Quick! Grab Sylvie!'

By the car she repeated Matthew's words.

'Guess what?' said Sylvie. 'Didn't you ask?'

'It's obvious.'

'Nothing's obvious,' said Sylvie. She tried to catch Claudia's eye, shaking her head and nodding at Anna.

'Belle's ill,' said Claudia. 'It's something really bad.'

They turned back to the quay where Matthew and Aunt Belle were outlined against the water. 'She's *paying* him,' whispered Claudia. 'That's awful. I thought he was doing it for old times' sake.'

At home, Belle sang as she coated the fish with breadcrumbs and fried them in a heavy skillet. 'There's nothing wrong with her at all,' Sylvie murmured to Anna. 'Don't worry.'

'I couldn't stand it if there was.'

Claudia listened to them from the end of the table. They could think what they liked. Aunt Belle *was* ill. She didn't need to ask. She'd known for ages.

She came down that night. Aunt Belle was dozing in her easy chair in the kitchen. Her glass was empty. 'Can we have a chat, Aunt Belle? Shall I fill your glass?'

'What do you want to talk about?' Belle's cheeks were deep crimson. Above them her hair was snowy. 'You seem more settled this time, Cloddie. Have you taken to Wilf a bit?'

'He's OK. I don't want to talk about Mum and Wilf, though.'
'Oh?'

'I want you to tell me about what it used to be like living here when you were young. Anna says you tell her all sorts of bits and pieces when you're practising together. I'm interested too. I'm not just being jealous. It was really nice hearing about your fishing trips. There's lots you've never told me.'

Belle yawned. 'What are you doing, Cloddie? Writing a family history or something?'

'I just want you to talk to me.' Claudia pulled up a stool. '– About yourself. I don't know why I've never asked you to before. I know you were married, for instance.'

Belle straightened herself up in her chair. 'Goodness, we are going back a long time! Perhaps you should fill my glass, dear. We'll be here half the night.'

When Claudia stood up her knees were quivering. 'I don't care how long we are.'

Sylvie and Anna woke early to twigs banging against the window. 'Gale!' mumbled Sylvie. 'Good job it didn't catch us at sea!'

'Wake her,' whispered Anna. 'I'm dying to know what Belle said. She won't mind if it's you. She'll just snap at me. She always thinks I'm making a fuss.'

Claudia listened to them from behind closed eyes. They'd known she was going down to talk to Belle last night. They'd practically bundled her down the stairs. But the conversation hadn't turned out to be anything she wanted to share with them. It hadn't really been a conversation at all – more a monologue. At first, Belle had been alert and happy. Some of her stories had been droll and they'd both laughed. After that, there had been a middle phase when she had become serious and her tales had taken on a cautionary flavour. By the end her eyes had been downcast, and her speech indistinct. She had asked Claudia to help her along to her bedroom and at the door she'd kissed her. 'Dear Cloddie, I'm afraid you got rather more than you bargained for . . .'

'Cloddie,' Sylvia was whispering. 'Did you speak to Aunt Belle?'

'What did she say?' said Anna. 'Did she tell you what's been wrong? You were ages.'

Claudia rolled over. 'She's OK.'

'Well, what were you talking about all that time?'

'Family stuff.'

'Did you tell her we thought she was different this time? Did you say we were worried?'

'Not exactly. She did all the talking. I couldn't suddenly interrupt and say, "Oh, by the way, we all think you've gone peculiar and Sylvie says you're becoming an alcoholic"!'

'You could have found out,' said Anna quietly. 'You could have put it another way.' She lay back. Shadows of the tossing branches outside shimmered over the ceiling. The wind was wild. 'I think you're hiding something, Cloddie. I think you're not telling us.'

For the first time, Aunt Belle appeared for breakfast in her dressing-gown. She leaned against the stove, watching their toast. 'Cloddie kept me up half the night,' she said to Anna and Sylvie. 'Or perhaps I kept her up half the night.'

'Lucky Cloddie,' said Anna. 'I wish I'd stayed up too.'

'Just old family stories, dear. Very boring for someone who's not actually related.'

Anna stared down at her cereal. 'I wish I was related to you. I wouldn't have been bored anyway.'

They lingered in the kitchen for most of the morning, talking about going out but reluctant to face the blast. 'You're getting under my feet,' said Belle unexpectedly. 'You'll like it when you get going. The sea's very exciting on days like this. It's not actually raining, you know. Do you good to get a blow.'

'She's got a guilty conscience,' said Claudia, catching up with the others at the gate. 'I think she just wants a rest. She's given me a fiver for chips at Wet Sands.'

'That's miles!' said Sylvie, gulping in the wind. 'She must really want us out of the way.'

'She says I can ring up if it's wet and she'll collect us in the car from wherever we are.'

'Big deal!'

'I think she's in pain,' said Anna. 'I don't think she want us to know.'

The Flat Fish at Wet Sands Bay was on the point of closing by the time they got there but the owner took pity on them. He pulled back the bolts and gave them left-over chips. 'It's going to pour,' he said. 'Where have you got to get to?'

The blue Ford pulled up with a jerk and Belle climbed out, clutching her coat around her. Claudia saw her first. 'She's here!' She collected their plates and carried them to the counter. 'Thanks for letting me use the phone. My aunt's here.'

They could see Belle's blurred shape through the patterned glass as she struggled with the door handle. The door flew open suddenly and she stumbled in on a gust of air, looking like an old brown bear. 'Have you paid?' she whispered to Claudia. 'Let's get going.'

The man at the counter eyed her suspiciously. 'You driving?' he asked. Belle ignored him. She fumbled in her pocket for a hanky and rubbed her nose with it as she bustled Anna and Sylvie out to the car.

Claudia stood at the counter with her five-pound note. 'That your aunt?' said the man. 'Has she had a drink?'

'No,' said Claudia. 'She's always like that. She's got a bad leg and the wind makes her dizzy.'

Outside, Belle was revving the car and preparing to swing it out into the stream of traffic. 'Careful!' said Claudia as she jumped in and the car lurched forward. 'We're all full of greasy chips!'

Sylvie said afterwards that she spent the whole journey with her eyes shut, praying for deliverance, as they tore along the narrow, twisty roads. Anna was never very willing to discuss the affair and if anyone else referred to it her eyes filled with tears. When the car at last swerved in through the gates and skidded to a halt outside the back door, Claudia, white with fright, turned on Aunt Belle. 'You're drunk, you stupid old bag! You could have killed us all off. We could all be lying out on the road like a pile of strawberry jam! You're blind *drunk*!'

11

They huddled beside the Aga, trembling and cupping their hands round mugs of the soup that Belle had left simmering. She was in her bedroom along the corridor. Claudia alone seemed clear-headed, ladling the soup and muttering, 'We could all be dead. Damn fool!'

Rain clouds blotted out the failing light and it was soon dark. The kitchen was warm and still. No one moved to switch on the lamp.

'Claudia!'

It was a low voice, very faint, coming from a distance. Claudia sprang to her feet. The call came again.

'Shall I go?' said Anna.

Claudia ignored her. She opened the kitchen door and disappeared down the unlit corridor.

'What d'you think's going on, Sylvie?' whispered Anna. 'Do you think she really was drunk?'

'Course she was.'

'But after all she's said . . . I don't believe it.'

Sylvie shrugged. 'No one's perfect.'

'She almost was. I'm not going to hold it against her.'

Along the corridor a door clicked and footsteps approached. They came as far as the hall, then the phone pinged and after a while they could hear Claudia's voice. When the receiver went down, the kitchen door opened and Claudia's head looked in at them. 'We're leaving. I've phoned Mum. She and Wilf will be here in two hours. We're travelling overnight.'

Anna's return threw Mrs Hackman into confusion. Ralph's friend was installed in her bedroom. He was enjoying himself. The Hackmans were enjoying having him. Everything was perfect. Anna wasn't expected back for three days.

'She can stay here, if you like,' Fern said on the phone, the morning after their journey. 'She and Sylvie have piled into Claudia's room with sleeping-bags. They're happy as Larry!' Aunt Belle was ill, she'd said. Nothing serious, but it had seemed best to bring the girls home at once.

Mrs Hackman dithered. Ralph's friend was a charming boy but obviously used to things being 'nice'. It would be better not to have to ask him to double up with Ralph. On the other hand there was Anna's practice and homework.

'She can practise her violin here,' said Fern, 'though we haven't got a piano. And she can do her homework.'

So Anna stayed. Sylvie was taken home to East Edge at lunchtime. Fern found Celia Lamont trimming round the flower-beds with a pair of edging shears. 'So you're Mrs Spark.' Mrs Lamont pulled off an old glove to shake hands. 'It's nice to put a face to the voice.'

'Fern,' said Fern. 'Or *Miss* Spark actually.'

'Oh yes, of course. I'm so sorry. It slipped my mind.'

Fern blinked. How could anyone forget that sort of thing? Claudia would never believe it. 'I'm afraid my aunt drove the girls in her car when she shouldn't have done. She takes painkillers most of the time and they make her pretty dozy. She felt horribly ashamed and sent for me to bring them home – fortunately I wasn't too far away.'

'How sad,' said Mrs Lamont. 'She's obviously such a kind woman.'

'She's got cancer,' said Fern. 'There's nothing much anyone can do. I haven't told Claudia. Belle wanted to carry on normally right to the bitter end. But I had my doubts about this visit. That's why I went down with them this time. I must say she seemed OK. Not chirpy, but coping. I thought it would be perfectly all right to leave them.'

Back at Candlemaker Row, without Sylvie, Anna could no longer ignore the rift that had opened between herself and Claudia. In the past they would both have been thrilled at the prospect of three days and nights together, but now it was obvious that Claudia couldn't be bothered with her. In fact, she seemed to be trying to pretend Anna wasn't there at all – practising her flute for hours, flopping about reading, and going early to bed.

'I know you didn't mean to be unkind to Aunt Belle,' Anna said from her sleeping-bag one night, 'when you called her a drunk old bag. She'll know you didn't mean it, too.'

'Is that so?'

'You just said it because you were so terrified.'

'If you say so.'

'I've written to her, have you? I posted it this afternoon. I said I didn't care about what happened. It was quite excusable.'

'I don't agree,' said Claudia. 'I don't think it's excusable at all for an old woman to get pissed in the middle of the afternoon and risk killing herself and three kids by rocketing down narrow lanes in a clapped-out wreck.'

In the darkness, Anna's voice shook. 'I don't get you, Cloddie. She wasn't drunk at all. It was her pills that made her woozy. I just want her to know we don't hold it against her.'

'I do hold it against her. She stank of drink. We could be dead and it would all be her fault.'

'But we still love her,' said Anna. 'Don't we? Well, I do. I don't suppose Sylvie does, really. But I do – don't you?'

Claudia stared at the strip of light along the bottom of the door. She could just make out the lump of Anna's mattress and sleeping-bag on the floor. She wanted to kick it. Sensitive, everyone called her, as if no one else had any feelings. 'God knows!' she muttered. 'I'm certainly not going to discuss my feelings for my relatives with you.'

It was a while before Anna spoke again, in a timid whisper. 'It's great being here with you, Cloddie. Mum would never have let me stay any other time. It's a really nice little house.'

'In a really grotty little street.'

'I wasn't going to say that. I wasn't even thinking it.'

'You'll be thinking it soon enough if any of the gangs come down here later, chucking cans around and peeing in the alleys. They bang on all the doors as they go past. You never know who they're going to bust in on.'

The lump on the floor curled itself into a tight ball. 'You're worried about Aunt Belle. I don't blame you.'

Claudia turned her face to the wall. 'I love Tod's,' Aunt Belle was saying. 'It never changes.' Claudia could see Belle's face again, as it had been that last night, deep red in the lamp-light. 'I like to think it'll always be here, peopled with relatives of mine. It's only ever had Sparks in it, of course. I like to think the wheel will turn full circle and times will be happy and prosperous like when your grandfather and I were children.' She'd talked on and on, cramming all her memories and hopes into that one night. 'If you're ever in any doubt about who you are and where you come from, Cloddie, "Tod's" is your answer.' If she'd been drunk then, it had been in a way that had made her warm and animated. It was much later that she had become completely exhausted and stumbled feebly down the passage on Claudia's arm.

'How did she seem when you stayed up with her the last night?' It was Anna's voice, intruding again, nosing into the things that were private. 'That was the last time any of us really saw her to talk to. She was awfully irritable next morning, wasn't she? I suppose if she hadn't stayed up half the night and worn herself out, nothing would have gone wrong. You were the last one to see her really.'

'She's not dead, you know.'

'I wish we could just go back and tell her we don't mind . . .'

'I shouldn't think your mum'll ever let you within a million miles of Tod's again.'

'I shan't tell her. I know your mum hasn't. She'll never know. She thinks Belle's great.'

'Aunt Belle will tell her herself. She'll write. She won't have you visiting under false pretences. Your mum'll hit the roof.'

'It'll depend how Belle explains it. There might be some reason . . .'

'She's dying,' said Claudia. 'That's the reason.'

Claudia was right about Belle writing. Letters reached the Hackmans and the Lamonts almost at once. Belle admitted her negligence. She offered no excuses, but apologized and thanked them for having entrusted their daughters to her care. She had enjoyed the girls' company, she said, but she wouldn't be inviting them to Tod's again. Mrs Lamont replied by return, accepting the apologies and thanking Belle for the good times she'd given Sylvie. Mrs Hackman's immediate response was to reach for the phone and spend half an hour gabbling into Belle's ear. What had happened? What was Belle's illness? Was there anything she could do? Of course Anna could come to Tod's again – any time she was asked. Anybody could make a mistake. 'Don't abandon us,' she pleaded. The line went crackly. Belle seemed to be saying something nice about Anna. When Mrs Hackman replaced the receiver she sat down and penned a lengthy epistle to Belle. These days she needed Belle's approval and support. Although they had known one another only a short time, an involved correspondence had sprung up between them. Mrs Hackman turned to Belle as to a mother and Belle responded. Mrs Hackman's pill-bottles were gathering dust along the top of the medicine cabinet.

Anna left Number Nine gladly, in no doubt at all about Claudia's hostility towards her. She felt light of heart and step, departing from Candlemaker Row with her violin and suitcase. She didn't expect ever to return and didn't care. No one would guess what went on in that little house when the doors and curtains were closed – how Claudia dominated the entire household with her moods. Mainly she was oppressively silent. If she spoke at all, it was only to launch an attack. Her thrusts were usually directed at Fern, but anyone present could find themselves set upon. 'She practically reduced me to a heap,' Anna told Sylvie in the basement at East Edge. 'She kept saying that Aunt Belle was dead on her feet, and she was forever pulling my mother to bits. She was vile the whole time, specially in the evenings. You should hear how she talks to her mother and Wilf. She hates them and they just sit there taking it.'

'I suppose people's worst side always comes out at home. She's not so bad at school, is she? Mum's always telling me to be nice to her. It must be awful living in that dump, not knowing if Wilf's going to move in any minute. And then there's Belle to worry about . . .'

'*Dying*, she told me.'

'Oh, she'd just be having you on. She's jealous of you and Belle.'

'I suppose she is. Not that she used to have one good word to say about her – and she's horrible about that last day, says Belle was drunk and it wasn't pills at all.'

'Well, we can try and be nice to her at school. We don't have to ask her home any more. And it doesn't sound as if she'll ever be asking us anywhere.'

Term started with the usual handing back of last term's tests, and results. For each subject the routine was the same. The teachers read out names and marks alphabetically but when the lists went up they were in order of merit. To Claudia's astonishment, her name headed three lists.

'What's been going on on the quiet, then?' said Sylvie. 'Who's turning into a big swot?'

Claudia laughed. 'Would you believe I did it without trying?'

Sylvie shook her head, but it was true. At the end of the previous term, Claudia had found herself invited less frequently to East Edge. She had suspected Sylvie of protecting Raymond's bruised feelings and, for her own part, had been relieved not to have to confront him. At home in the evenings, almost without realizing it, she had spent hours on her homework simply because there was nothing else to do. Fern was either swotting for the Open University or watching television with Wilf. There was no garden to speak of and there were no friends nearby. Apart from flute practice and the reading she'd begun to do for Wilf, there were no diversions.

'She's done it to get back at me,' muttered Anna. She was standing by the notice-board, pinch-faced. 'She's had it in for me ever since Tod's. You'd think the whole thing was my fault.'

'Don't be an idiot,' said Sylvie. 'We did the tests before that.'

'Mum'll get in a state. She'll think I'm going down the drain.'

'You're top in Art,' said Sylvie, 'and Music. You can't call that going down the drain.'

Claudia stood back, watching them – Sylvie clucking, Anna twisting her hands and face just like when everyone thought she had wet her knickers in Primary One. 'For God's sake, shut up, Anna! I never gave you a thought. But thanks for the suggestion.

I'll have a go at Art and Music this term – see if I can scrub you off the map altogether.'

'You see?' Anna sobbed as Claudia walked away. 'That's what she thinks of me.'

Mrs Hackman took the news of Anna's test defeats with resolute calm. 'Belle has always said you're bound to go in for Music. There's absolutely no point in thinking you'll go on being top in everything else too. I've been expecting this to happen. You've had a pretty good run but now I suppose it's just an indication that we should start specializing. You can plug away at your other subjects in a more leisurely way and we'll step up on the music practice. Belle predicted this. Aren't we lucky she takes such an interest?'

'There's Claudia,' said Anna. 'She's bound to put her first.'

'She thinks Claudia's like herself. Self-sufficient, she means. I must say I don't see any other similarity. But it's us she worries about. She thinks you're gifted. She thinks you need very special handling.'

'Did she say so?'

'More or less. Reading between the lines. She thinks the pressure should be taken off.'

Anna didn't notice any conspicuous release of pressure as the term advanced. Five hundred pounds was spent on a new violin and music practice was almost doubled, her mother crouching beside her with renewed fervour. Other subjects received concentrated attention in any time that was left – sufficient to keep Anna in the top half of the class but no more. Her position as leader in just about everything was well and truly usurped – notably by Claudia, whose sudden intense interest in school-work brought unexpected peace to Number Nine. She discovered Wilf to be remarkably well informed on a variety of subjects and they sat on at the table after supper with Claudia's books spread in front of them while Fern washed up or slipped off to read on her own. The test results had come as a revelation to Claudia. This would show Aunt Belle. 'Anna's very talented,' she'd said that last night. 'You don't get many like her.'

'She's been pushed. We could all be . . .'

Belle had shaken her head. 'No, Cloddie, we couldn't. It's

something you're born with. I just hope that mother of hers isn't going to smother it.'

'You must think I'm a dud or something.'

Aunt Belle had reached out and ruffled her hair. 'I dare say, in the world's terms, you're more of a winner than Anna. What she's got needs optimum conditions to blossom. She'll need all the help she can get, poor mite. I suppose that's our rôle, Cloddie. Towers of strength!' She laughed and repeated herself. 'Towers of strength . . . !'

'Claudia's turning out to be rather clever, isn't she?' Wilf said to Fern one night.

'Her father was very bright.'

'You're no fool yourself. I don't see there's any need to look further than that.'

Fern smiled.

'When are you going to tell her?' said Wilf suddenly.

'What's the hurry? You can see how she's beginning to come round to you. I don't think we should take her by surprise.'

'*Surprise*! I've been around ages. She's had enough hints dropped.'

Fern shook her head. 'I don't think she's giving us a thought these days,' she said calmly. 'She's preoccupied with her school-work and I think that's how it should be. I don't think she ought to be feeling all unsettled by us. I like to see her getting on.'

'She's seeing sense,' grunted Wilf. 'She knows there'll be O levels in no time. And I bet she knows perfectly well we want to get married. She just thinks you'll never bring it to a head if she doesn't mention it. She's stringing us both along. She's quite clever enough for that. You should tell her.'

'Not yet,' said Fern firmly. 'And don't you. We've seen where that gets us.'

The phone call came as no surprise to Fern. Since Easter she had been half expecting it. She was glad now that she had never succeeded in rousing Claudia to a proper regard for Aunt Belle.

She left a note on the kitchen table. Belle was in Cranwick

Infirmary. Wilf was driving her down. Mrs Lamont would be very happy for Claudia to stay at East Edge, if she wanted to.

It was a clammy afternoon in May. Claudia's hand shook as she reread the letter. She sat down on the edge of one of the kitchen stools and shivered. 'Towers of strength,' Belle had said, and now she was toppling over and all the people who were leaning against her were about to come crashing down too. Claudia jumped to her feet. In the hall she twice dialled the Tod Pool number but there was no reply. She thought of Anna. She hadn't spoken to her for days, but Anna loved Aunt Belle. She'd said so.

'It's Cloddie, Anna. Aunt Belle's in hospital.'

'Oh . . .'

'It must be serious. Mum's dashed off to see her. I think she's dying, Anna. I'm sure she is.'

'You've been saying that for ages and she hasn't died yet. Old people get things. It's probably nothing at all.' Anna's voice was guarded. 'Why did you ring me?'

'I thought you'd want to know. I'm in a state – don't you care?'

'Why should I care about you all of a sudden?'

'About Aunt Belle, then. Leave me out of it. She's dying, I tell you.'

'I don't believe you. I had a letter from her yesterday. She said she was hoping I'd go in the summer. On my own – or maybe with Mum. I told her you and I weren't very friendly any more.'

'Why did you tell her that?'

'Look, I've got to go, Claudia. I'm right in the middle of practice. Phone Sylvie.'

After that, Claudia sat alone at the living-room window. She didn't phone Sylvie or go to stay at East Edge. 'Poor old Belle,' Sylvie would say. 'You were right, then. Poor old thing, getting iller and iller all on her own. Don't panic the Hackmans.' Sylvie was useless. She didn't know anything . . . It was dark by the time Fern rang. Before she picked up the phone, Claudia stood for a second just looking at it.

Claudia woke in the chair by the window. She was stiff and cold. 'Promise me you'll go to the Lamonts',' Fern had said. But she'd stayed at home, watching the dark street. No need to wonder any more how ill Belle was, or if she'd get better . . . Claudia brushed her hair and went into the kitchen. Through the wall she could hear a radio. More squatters. Today was her flute lesson. There was going to be a French test. No one would be bothering about an old woman in Norfolk snuffing it . . . only Anna.

At a quarter past eight, Claudia pushed her bike out into the street and cycled to Winchester Road. She stopped on the corner and sat, arms folded, balancing with one foot on the kerb. Anna saw her the minute she rounded the bend. There was no way of dodging her. Claudia was getting off her bike and advancing slowly.

'What d'you want, Cloddie?'

'I knew you'd want to know. I thought I should tell you in person. It's bad news.'

Anna stopped dead. 'What is it?'

'Aunt Belle died yesterday. I told you she would, didn't I?'

'It is true, Cloddie? Are you sure?'

'Get your mum to ring Tod's. My mum's there. She'll tell her.'

Anna stared at her for a moment longer, then whimpered, snatched up her school-bag, and dashed back the way she had come.

'We knew something was up, didn't we?' said Sylvie at school. 'I feel really sad, don't you? That business at Easter was a rotten end.'

'She should've told me how ill she was,' said Claudia. 'I hate being treated like a kid.'

'We'd better be careful what we say to Anna. I think it'd be best if your mother broke it – to Mrs Hackman.'

'I've told Anna already. I went round by Winchester Road this morning. I don't think Anna'll come to school. They make such a flipping fuss. You'd think Belle was *their* relative.'

'That was mean, Cloddie – just knocking them over the head with it.'

'*Mean*! I went round there at the bloody crack of dawn, didn't I? – just so Anna wouldn't find out at school. I knew she'd pass out. I don't call that mean. I call it very kind and considerate!' Claudia cackled indignantly.

Sylvie's blood ran cold. It wasn't right, laughing like that. 'Are you all alone at home?' she asked, forcing the conversation on. 'Mum was half expecting you to come and stay. Your mum phoned.'

Claudia darted her a bright, sideways glance. 'What about Ray? You'd hate me to come really, wouldn't you?' She went away whistling, reminding Sylvie of the flute-playing she'd heard through the window in Candlemaker Row. Perhaps she should go round there again after school. They could cook tea like last time, and talk about Belle. Sylvie opened her locker and began to sort out books for the morning's lessons. She wouldn't be going anywhere near Candlemaker Row at the end of the day. She knew that.

12

In the distress of the moment, there were several words of caution and advice that Fern forgot to pass on to Mrs Smee when she phoned her from Tod's. Mrs Smee sounded so practical and capable. She'd been a teacher most of her life, she reminded Fern. There wasn't much she couldn't handle. She would value the opportunity of getting to grips with Claudia. Slippery customers, these teenagers. She told Fern that, sad as the circumstances were, she welcomed them in a way. They would give her the chance to get close to Claudia. There would be things Claudia would want to say. She would need a shoulder to lean on.

'Wilf's not here,' said Claudia in astonishment. Mrs Smee was standing on the doorstep in evening sunshine, a suitcase at her feet.
'I'm not looking for Wilf, dear. Didn't your mother explain?'
'I've only just got in. She hasn't phoned or anything.'
'Never mind.' Mrs Smee picked up the suitcase and stepped briskly into the hall. 'I'll take my things straight upstairs, dear. I'm to have your mother's room. You put the kettle on.'
Claudia stood in the kitchen, listening to the sounds overhead. If Mrs Smee only knew what her dear son had been getting up to in that very room – in that very bed. What the hell was she doing here? How long was she staying? Already she was trotting back down the narrow stairs . . . Mrs Smee came into the kitchen in soft leather slippers and a gingham overall. Her hair was cropped shorter than ever. She sat down at the table, pushed her glasses up over the top of her head and rubbed her eyes. 'I wish they'd managed to get in touch with you before I arrived, dear. The fact is, they've decided to stay on for a bit – to see to the funeral and sort the house out. Your mother phoned this morning. We thought it might be nice if I came down to keep you company. It'll just be

for a few days. To tell you the truth, as we're shortly to be related, I thought it'd be rather nice for us to get to know one another properly . . .'

Claudia turned round slowly with the teacups. Mrs Smee was sitting there, three yards away, grinning like a skull. Nothing was real any more. Claudia felt the weight go out of her arm as the apparition took a cup from her. She pulled up a stool and lowered herself on to it. The skull talked on and on, teeth clacking, bones rattling. Claudia sat absolutely still as crystal truths formed in her head. They had been full of lies and deceit, Aunt Belle and Fern. Belle had sat up most of a night assuring Claudia that she was telling her all there was to know about herself and Tod's and all the Sparks – but she hadn't said she was dying. Fern had denied that there was any thought in her head of marrying Wilf, but they had obviously been hotting up their seedy little romance behind her back and had already made wedding plans . . . And here sat this stringy old woman, drinking her tea at the kitchen table and announcing that they were practically the same flesh and blood. Claudia started to laugh. She doubled up and giggled till tears ran down her face.

'That's just what you need, dear,' said Mrs Smee, looking concerned. 'You go on and have a good cry.'

'Good laugh, you mean,' choked Claudia. 'Haven't had such a good one in years!'

Fern and Wilf were away for a week. On the afternoon of their return Mrs Smee and Claudia hovered at the window, watching for the car. They had passed the week amicably but without holding, in Mrs Smee's opinion, a single significant conversation. 'You'll be glad to have your mum back,' she said, making a final bid. 'I expect you're very close.'

'Not specially.'

'It'll be a change for you, having a man about the house.'

'Not really,' said Claudia. 'Mum's always had someone around.'

A tightness crept over Mrs Smee's face. 'Oh, well, I expect it'll all work out in the end,' she mumbled.

Fern and Wilf brought with them a boot-load of odds and ends from Tod's. Valuables that were asking to be pinched, Fern said. Neighbours were keeping an eye on the house but it was common knowledge in the village that it was empty. The funeral had publicized that.

'What was it like?' asked Claudia.

'Packed. You'd never believe Belle had so many friends. Of course, she'd lived there most of her life and she was very helpful to people – specially old folk. There were dozens of them there. The vicar was very good. He knew she wasn't religious. He didn't dwell on Heaven or anything. But I was glad we didn't just make do with the crematorium service . . . The Hackmans were there, of course.'

'The *Hackmans*!'

'Just Anna and her mother. Surely Anna told you!'

'She hasn't been at school.'

'They slipped in at the back, didn't they, Wilf? A really forlorn sight. They looked shattered. They gave an enormous spray of flowers. Must've cost the earth.'

'Bloody Anna, poking her nose in . . . *I* should've been there.'

'Belle wouldn't have wanted it, Cloddie. She wouldn't have wanted Anna there either, I'm sure. She always said a funeral was no place for a child.'

They unwrapped the things from Tod's – a mirror with gilt Cupids round the edge, vases and china figurines, pewter and tarnished silver mugs – and stood them in a corner of the room. 'They don't look right here, do they?' said Claudia. 'They look really old and musty – just like the rest of Tod's.'

Fern glanced over her shoulder at Wilf. He nodded. 'Actually, Cloddie, I might as well not beat about the bush. There was a will. You've done rather well.'

'What d'you mean?'

'Belle left Tod's to you,' said Fern. 'The house – she wanted you to have it.'

Claudia stared at Fern. Slowly she went bright red in the face, then sprang to her feet and bolted from the room. They could hear her dragging her bike outside, then the front door banged and they caught a glimpse of her head flashing past the window.

'She's been good as gold all week,' said Mrs Smee. 'No bother at all. I think you've taken her by surprise.'

'It's not my fault,' said Fern, her eyes filling. 'I had nothing to do with it. I didn't know how she'd take it. We can always sell it, I suppose.'

'I'll take you back to my flat, Mother,' whispered Wilf, guiding Mrs Smee into the hall. 'Fern's been under a lot of strain. Aunt Belle was like a second mother to her. She and Claudia need to be alone together.'

Claudia pedalled furiously as far as the outskirts of the town and joined the ring road. It was raining again. Her tyres hissed. Spray flew from the wheels of passing cars. Headlights, pricking through the dusk, prompted her to stop and turn on her own lights. 'Tod's means everything to me,' Belle had mumbled late in the night, flopping back in her chair. 'Solid good memories. I shall die happy if I know it will always stay in our family.'

'I thought things were sad. Specially after the accident.'

'Sad for me and Fern. We've been the unlucky ones. But not for all the Sparks who lived here before that and not for any future Sparks. You wouldn't say Tod's was sad now, would you? You're not telling me you've brought your friends down here because it's a grim, dreary place? You know what Tod's is. You're a Spark.'

'Half,' murmured Claudia.

With a massive effort, Belle had reared up in her chair. 'Half by blood and wholly by upbringing. You're rooted here like all the rest of us. Make no mistake about that. You've been a part of this house all your life. Longer, even – Fern brought you here even before you were born. This was where she came when she was pregnant with you. She was quite right.'

'Yes,' said Claudia, alarmed by Belle's bulging eyes. 'I know the sort of place it is. That's why I keep coming back myself.' It had been the right answer. Belle had subsided into her cushions.

Fern sat up with a jump. There was thumping and bumping in the hall. It was the middle of the night. She must have dropped off on the sofa.

'Is Tod's actually mine this minute?' Claudia said, bursting in through the door. She perched on the arm of the sofa, taut and alert.

'I think it's to be in trust. I think I'm supposed to be vaguely in charge till you're twenty-one or something.'

'Oh, I see. It's not really mine at all, then.'

'It is – or will be. Belle's intentions were perfectly clear. Tod's is definitely yours.'

'Why didn't she leave it to you? I thought it was to be your nest egg.'

'I think she thought I might make some other future for myself.'

'Wilf, you mean. I know you're going to marry him – any minute, by the sound of it. Mrs Smee told me.'

'Oh.' Fern dropped her head in her hands. 'I really was going to tell you, Cloddie. I was waiting for the right moment.'

'She's dead against it, you know. She had higher hopes for her only son.'

Fern sighed. 'You're lying, Cloddie. Save your breath. She's been dying for Wilf to marry. She was really disappointed at Christmas when we didn't get engaged.'

'Well, I'm not going to live at Tod's with the pair of you, if that's the little scheme. Did you and Belle hatch this up? – she'd leave the house to me when I'm grown up, but in the meantime we all live there together. Is it supposed to be a way of keeping me sweet? – dressing it up as if something special's being done for me. Actually what's happened is that Belle has handed over Tod's to you as a big fat wedding present. Well, you won't get me down there. I'm glad I've seen the back of it.'

Anna returned to school pale and a good deal thinner. She'd had a sort of asthma after the funeral, she said. It had come on in the church. She'd kept thinking of Belle's body boxed up in the coffin, not breathing. And then her own lungs had seized up.

'Serve you right,' said Claudia. 'You aren't family. You shouldn't have gone at all.'

'Your mum said Belle would've been pleased.'

'That's not what she told me.'

'Course Belle would've been pleased,' said Sylvie. 'She liked you – because of the music.'

Anna nodded. 'Actually, she did something rather amazing. She left me her piano. And all her music.' She sobbed suddenly. 'I'm sorry. Let's talk about something else.'

'As a matter of fact,' said Claudia, 'she's left the house and everything in it to me. You've got a damn nerve claiming anything. You've already hogged most of her attention over the last few months. You and your mad mother. The least you can do is keep your hands off her property.'

Anna turned rigid. Her head jutted forward on her thin neck. 'You mean pig! You monster!' she shrilled. 'She loved that house. Heaven knows why she's left it to you. But the piano she left to me and there's nothing you can do about it. Mum got a solicitor's letter yesterday. She's having it removed as soon as possible. We want part of Belle with us.'

Claudia shrugged suddenly and turned away. 'Have it then. You could have had the whole lot of her for all I care. I certainly don't want that old dump.'

13

'Purely out of interest,' began Claudia, turning from the sink and fixing Wilf with an innocent gaze, 'do you intend to beget further offspring upon my mother? *After* marrying her, of course.' She had waited for this moment. The wedding was barely a month off. Following Belle's last advice, Fern had raced ahead with plans. 'Don't hang about having an engagement,' Belle had said. 'If your own mind is made up, get straight on with it. Don't prolong the agony for Cloddie. She won't like it, but she'll adjust. It's what she needs.'

Wilf blinked. 'Ah,' he said, 'what's all this about?'

'Will it be your intention – when the two of you are man and wife together, as they say – to impregnate my mother?'

Wilf closed his book carefully. Of late, Claudia had been cool and detached, giving the impression that, as far as she was concerned, neither Belle's death nor the imminent marriage of her mother was of much consequence. She had brushed aside Fern's reassurances. 'We'll just carry on here,' Fern had said. 'There's plenty of room. Life won't change that much.' Claudia had looked blank. 'Fine,' was all she'd said.

'I don't really think,' said Wilf now, 'that this is a suitable topic for you and me. But I do assure you that I won't be having any intentions in that direction that aren't shared by Fern.'

Claudia gave a little laugh. 'No need to be so embarrassed, Wilf. Mind you, I don't think babies about the place would be a good idea, do you? The house is too small and Mum's no good with kids.'

'She seems to like looking after the American children.'

'Well, she doesn't like being lumbered with her own. I can vouch for that. She hated having me.'

'Rubbish,' said Wilf. 'She just wished you had a father, that's all. She felt she hadn't given you the best start.'

Claudia smiled. 'You can say that again. Still, she wouldn't need to feel that now – in the case of other children, I mean.'

'Quite.'

'So you might very well decide to father a little Smee? Ma and Pa Smee and Baby Smee. The three Smees.'

'We shall be three without me doing any more than step-fathering,' said Wilf. 'Do you think it'd be nice if we all had the same name? We'd be a proper family.'

'Who're you kidding?' said Claudia with another little laugh. 'What have names got to do with it? This'll never be a proper family as long as I'm around.'

Wilf moved into Number Nine a week before the wedding. He had sold his own flat and had nowhere else to go. 'Seedy as ever,' Claudia remarked to Fern as he trudged back and forth, unpacking his possessions from the car and looking for places to put them in his new home. 'Thank God you're not wearing white on Saturday. I couldn't take it.'

On the Friday evening, Mrs Smee arrived in a black feathery hat she had bought for the ceremony. People had gawped at her on the train, she said, but there had been no other way of carrying it. 'Don't push Cloddie out of her bed, just for me,' she said to Fern, but Claudia insisted she have it. She admired Mrs Smee's breezy competence. You'd never guess she was seventy. You could tell nobody would ever get the better of her. She would never have got herself in Fern's sort of mess. Claudia wondered where Wilf would sleep now – surely not in Fern's room, with his mother in the house.

After supper, Fern and Wilf went round to The English Rose to organize the seating plan for their reception lunch, and Claudia and Mrs Smee found themselves alone in the living-room. 'How do you feel about having Wilf for a stepfather?' said Mrs Smee.

'Fine.'

'He's looking forward to it.'

Claudia nodded. 'Mum's been a bit lonely, stuck at home with me. It's nice she's met someone.' She excused herself on the grounds of homework and went upstairs. Mrs Smee's case was open on her bed. In Fern's room the smell was different already.

A suit of Wilf's was hanging on the back of the door. Near the bed, a pair of his brown lace-up shoes stood side by side with sandals of Fern's.

Mrs Smee heard the click of the front door and reached the window in time to see Claudia slipping away into the dusk. A youth, passing by on the pavement outside, objected to the sight of her peeping face and jerked his head violently. A roll of grey spittle began to slither down the glass. Mrs Smee returned to her chair, shaken. Surely Wilf wouldn't bring up children of his own in Candlemaker Row. It might be too late to save Claudia. But if there should be more . . .

When Claudia came in at eleven o'clock, Fern was alone in the living-room, stitching the hem of her cream-coloured wedding-dress. Cream tights and shoes were laid out beside her, and a pale hat trimmed with shiny red cherries. 'Where've you been? Do you want me to check over your clothes? Why don't you bring them down? Hang them with mine and we'll know where everything is.'

'Where's Wilf?'

'In bed. He thought we might want a last evening to ourselves. Where've you been?'

'Out.'

'You're always out. Where do you go?'

'Just walking. Sometimes cycling.'

'You don't seem to go over to Sylvie's much any more.'

'Her brother wrecked that. Anyway, Sylvie likes Anna best now.'

'Threesomes are tricky. Don't worry, they'll be all over you tomorrow.'

'It'll be weird without Aunt Belle. Sometimes I think she's not dead at all. It wouldn't surprise me in the least if she turned up.'

Fern gazed sadly at her stitching. 'I wish she could. I shall be trying not to think about her. For Wilf's sake, I don't want to look a misery. Belle would have enjoyed it all so much . . .'

'Quite often I forget she's dead. I just think she's down at Tod's as usual.'

'Oh, Cloddie, she's dead all right. If you'd seen her in the hospital . . . Maybe you should have come to the funeral . . .'

'She shouldn't have left me the house.'

'Why not? It was nothing to do with Wilf and me, you know. I didn't have any secrets with Belle apart from her illness. We didn't want you to know about that. She kept hoping she'd get better, and you and your pals cheered her up. She never said a word to me about her will – only what you knew too, that we were getting everything. Leaving the house specifically to you seems to have been a last-minute idea. She only did it after your Easter visit. She must have been making up her mind while you were there.'

'She was trying to make me be a Spark. She dinned it into me most of one night about Tod's being a family house. I suppose she knew you were going off with Wilf. I was her last hope.'

'I think she thought you liked the place,' murmured Fern. 'I think she thought you thought it was special.'

'Well, I don't. I never did. She was always ramming it down my throat – the Spark ancestral home and all that. I'm not a Spark at all.' Claudia's voice was rising. 'I'm what my father is. No one ever thinks of him.'

'Shhh,' warned Fern. 'Don't cause a fuss tonight, of all nights. Of course you're a Spark. You're my daughter, aren't you? Anyway, if you don't fancy it, think of yourself as just Claudia, Cloddie, whatever you like – it doesn't matter.'

'It matters to me!' shrieked Claudia. 'It's never mattered to you. You think I'm some sort of clone you've sliced off yourself. But I'm half someone else. I don't know who.'

Fern was on her feet, chin wobbling. She waved her long sewing scissors in front of Claudia's face. 'Clear off, you little bitch! You're not wrecking my bloody wedding day. We've had fourteen bloody years on your terms. Now it's my turn – and you'd better get something straight in your head, once and for all. Either you buckle down and fit in or you get out. Is that clear?' She straightened up, catching sight of someone in the doorway. Her face crumpled and the scissors dropped on to the sofa. Claudia looked round. Mrs Smee was standing in the hall. She pointed at Claudia. 'Bedtime, Miss. Upstairs and brush your teeth.'

Claudia delayed in the bathroom for as long as she reasonably could. When she came down, Fern and Mrs Smee were arranging the sofa for her. They stood by the fire as she climbed into her sleeping-bag. 'Goodnight, Cloddie,' said Mrs Smee, kissing her for the first time. Fern left the room last. She turned the light out, then crept back to the sofa. 'I'm sorry, Cloddie. It's wedding nerves. Try to understand.'

'Is Wilf sleeping with you tonight?' whispered Claudia. 'With his mother in the house! She'll think you're a real tramp.'

Fern had not realized the extent to which Claudia's friendships with Anna and Sylvie had broken down when she'd suggested inviting them to her reception lunch. 'You'll be bored to tears, Cloddie. It'll be better if you've got pals of your own. Wilf thinks so too.' Claudia had raised no objection, so Anna and Sylvie had been added to the guest list and had eventually accepted their invitations, curious to see how the event turned out and wondering if Claudia, influenced by a new climate of love and romance at home, could possibly be proffering an olive branch. They made their way to The English Rose together at eleven forty-five and promptly disappeared into the powder-room. 'I'm nervous,' said Anna, watching Sylvie apply gloss to her lips and some green shadow to her eyelids. 'I wonder why she asked me. She's been awful to me for ages.'

'She hasn't got any other friends,' said Sylvie. 'It was us or no one.'

'Well, I'm surprised she asked anyone, then. She doesn't seem to want friends nowadays. Mum's quite pleased about that, of course. She could never stand the Sparks – apart from Aunt Belle. And now Belle's dead, she can hardly bear to think of the other two.'

Sylvie giggled. 'Shut up, Anna. Someone'll hear you. I'm surprised your mum let you come today if that's how she goes on.'

'Partly for Belle's sake. Belle liked Wilf. She always hoped he'd marry Fern. And Mum was very impressed with Wilf herself, that time he picked us all up to take us to Tod's. Anyway, she knows she'll never get the chance of having lunch here. She wants me to tell her what it's like. And she wants me to try and meet Wilf's mother. She's a bit nosy about her.'

'She'll be wanting to know if there's money about,' said Sylvie. 'She'll be really sick if the Sparks have landed on their feet.'

'It's just ordinary curiosity,' said Anna huffily. 'Mum's perfectly OK.'

'I thought you said she was all twitchy again.' Anna had reported the reappearance of pill bottles and extra homework.

'She misses Belle. Belle used to calm her down.'

'How's she expecting you to do in the exams?'

'I dread to think.' Examinations were approaching – important ones which would determine the banding in individual subjects for the following year.

Claudia was at the reception desk, making enquiries for them. Her dress was deep pink and she was wearing matching shoes and holding a bouquet of tiny roses. Her eyes were very bright and her black hair curled tightly over her head, like lamb's wool. 'There you are!' She jumped between them and linked her arms through theirs. 'We've got a table all to ourselves for lunch. It's fantastic!' She marched them to the dining-room, which was dotted with round tables of varying sizes, each with a floor-length white cloth and centrepiece of tiny forget-me-nots. 'Everyone's in the bar,' she said. 'But I wanted you to see where we were going to sit.' Their table was by a window. Small white cards, propped against starched napkins, were printed with their names in silver. Sylvie and Anna grinned. 'It's great, Cloddie!' They followed her to the bar, making hopeful signs to one another behind her back.

Wilf and Fern were receiving guests and presents. They stood in a corner of the bar, an attractive couple of equal height; he dapper and slim in a grey striped suit, his wiry hair cut close to his head and his sharp eyes dancing; she fragile, too white-skinned for her pale dress, but stylish in the hat and shoes. 'They're a knock-out, Clod! They really are,' whispered Sylvie. 'So are you. Really, really smart. Must've cost the earth.'

'Wilf's quite rich, I think,' said Claudia, smoothing her skirt. 'He insisted on buying this – it was fifty pounds.'

'*Fifty*!' Anna reached out to touch the fabric but thought better of it. Her hand dropped to her side. 'It's lovely.'

At the bar, Claudia ordered drinks and brought them back on a small tray. 'Vodka! The barman never said a word. I thought we should try. Aunt Belle would approve.'

They sat down in a row along a padded window-seat and sipped from their glasses, giggling quietly and whispering about the guests as they filed in.

'What's that you've got hold of?' said Mrs Smee, advancing in her black hat. 'Lemonade?'

Sylvie nodded.

'Course it's not!' said Claudia. 'I thought we should all try vodka on a special day like this.'

Mrs Smee's eyes and nose were sharp, like Wilf's. 'Introduce me to your friends, Claudia.' She pulled up a chair and sat facing them while Claudia presented Anna and Sylvie.

Sylvie smiled politely and said, 'Nice to meet you.' She could see that this old bat had decided to nip any nonsense in the bud. She disapproved of the vodka. Perhaps she disapproved of Claudia too. But they'd be able to shake her off once they moved through to the dining-room.

Lunch was the suave, delectable affair that Mrs Hackman had assured Anna it would be. In the kitchen, the proprietor himself was attending to sauces. The three girls sat round their table, drinking chilled wine. Mrs Smee was miles away, on the other side of the room, sharing a table with Wilf and Fern and their closest friends. With a quick gulp Claudia emptied her glass. She beckoned to a passing waiter. 'Could you bring more wine?' she said. 'Could you leave a bottle on the table? I'm the daughter of the bride.'

'Cloddie!' whispered Anna as the waiter turned smoothly on his heel. 'I don't think you should've done that.'

'I'll do what I bloody like. When it's your mother's wedding, you can call a few tunes.'

'I didn't mean anything,' mumbled Anna as the waiter returned.

'Just the two of us, thank you,' said Claudia, indicating Sylvie and herself. 'Our friend's had enough, I think.'

The waiter filled the two glasses and went away leaving the bottle on the table.

Sylvie nudged Claudia. 'Give her a bit,' she whispered. 'Go on. She didn't mean anything.'

Claudia lifted the bottle and filled Anna's glass. 'I don't suppose Belle would ever have given you a drop if she'd known your parents had signed the pledge. But it seems a shame to waste all that practice.'

'I think she did know, actually,' said Anna. 'Thanks. Honestly, it's great here! Wilf really knows how to do things properly.'

'What makes you think it's all Wilf's doing? Mum and he made all the arrangements together.'

'She looks lovely,' said Sylvie, trying to reach Anna's foot under the table. 'She's ethereal!'

Anna sipped eagerly at her glass. 'Wilf looks just like you. It's the curly hair. You could easily be his daughter. People will never think anything else – specially if you change your name.'

Claudia turned back to the table. She'd been watching Wilf with something approaching approval. If there had to be a bloke round the house, she'd been thinking, perhaps Wilf wasn't actually the worst. At least he was neat and clean – though she'd never call him good-looking, with that shiny, pointed conk. 'What the hell makes you think I'd change my name? I'd rather die than pass myself off as the issue of that pair.'

At the next table, heads turned and then converged over the forget-me-nots. 'They heard,' said Anna, blushing deeply. 'They're whispering about us.'

'Whisper away!' said Claudia loudly.

'Here's the next course,' said Sylvie. 'Mind your elbows.'

They sat back in silence as the waiters leaned over their plates. Claudia breathed deeply. 'Smells nice,' she said. Sylvie watched as she picked up her cutlery and began to eat. What was it about Claudia? Why should she and Anna be on tenterhooks all the time? Really she was a spoilt cow, making them so jittery, ruining their meal.

'Wouldn't it be perfect if Belle was here?' Anna was saying. 'To tell you the truth, I can quite easily believe she is. She'd be over on your mum's table, wouldn't she? If you don't actually look, you can pretend she is. I wonder why you're not on that table, Cloddie? You should be with the family, shouldn't you?'

'Mum was under the impression I'd rather be with you.'

'If you've got to believe Belle's here, why not just pretend she's looking down from Heaven?' said Sylvie.

'I sort of see her quite often, as a matter of fact,' said Anna. 'Every time I play her piano, for a start.'

Claudia put down her knife and fork. She leaned her elbows carefully on the table, perched her chin on her hands and stared across at Anna. 'What exactly do you mean? What on earth are you on about?'

'I suppose it sounds mad,' babbled Anna, loading her fork and popping it in her mouth, 'but I often get a real feeling that she's beside me. Perhaps you do too. It doesn't frighten me at all. It seems the most natural thing in the world.'

'I never get the feeling she's anywhere near me,' said Claudia tartly. 'How do you explain that?'

Anna fiddled nervously with her glass. 'I don't mean literally, Cloddie. It's just a feeling I get. It's nothing. I suppose I just invent it. I can't bear to think she's gone for ever.'

'Well, she has,' said Claudia. She picked up her cutlery and began to eat again. 'Mum said she looked terrible in hospital. And she saw the corpse later. Belle was dead all right. And she wasn't religious, you know. So there'll be no second life coming up for her and no cosy visitations from her spirit for you. You saw the coffin at the crematorium, didn't you? You should know as well as anyone how dead she is.'

To Sylvie's dismay, tears welled up in Anna's eyes. As she watched, they overflowed, ran down her face and dropped on to the edge of the dinner plate. 'For God's sake,' she groaned at Claudia. 'Did you have to set her off?'

'She doesn't need to take any notice of me. If she thinks Belle's watching over her, she's probably right. Much more likely she'd be guardian angel to Anna than me. They're welcome to each other.'

They lapsed into silence and gradually the heads at the next table stopped turning in their direction. As the meal ended, they turned instead, expectantly, to Wilf who stood, outlined against the opposite window, to deliver an elegant little speech in praise of Fern and Claudia. He spoke in witty bursts, smiling at his friends, bending down to Fern every now and again. He wanted to toast the bridesmaid, he said, at last, Claudia, his chief literary adviser and now his stepdaughter. Claudia tried to focus on him. His voice had taken on an echoing quality. It seemed to be coming from miles away, across aeons of time. Around her, people were rising to their feet. 'Claudia!' they were murmuring. 'The bridesmaid.' Anna and Sylvie joined in.

'Are you going to call him Dad, or what?' whispered Anna as they sat down again.

This time, Sylvie's foot did make contact. 'Shut up!' she mouthed. 'Are you drunk or something?'

Claudia was reaching for her glass. Things were receding fast. It was harder and harder to be sure of what anyone was saying . . .

Claudia could never recall precisely when Wilf and Fern departed from The English Rose or if she stood with the group in the doorway, waving them off. She rather thought that she did. And she thought she remembered Anna and Sylvie, with boxes of confetti, racing along the road after Wilf's car, but she didn't think she ran with them, and she had no recollection of seeing them again. She went home on foot, her arm firmly hitched through Mrs Smee's, her teeth clenched. She made it into the hall of Number Nine and, as Mrs Smee turned to close the front door, her knees turned to jelly, her jaw dropped and she was helplessly sick on the floor. She looked up through watery eyes to see Mrs Smee leaning against the door with her arms folded. 'Well, at least we got you home,' was all she said.

Later she came upstairs with a towel and a bucket and sat on the edge of Claudia's bed. Claudia lay on her side with her eyes closed. 'I'm all right,' she mumbled. She heard Mrs Smee sigh and felt the shift of her weight on the mattress.

'You won't believe this, but you've been uppermost in everyone's mind for a long time,' said Mrs Smee. 'Wilf thinks very highly of you, you know. He'll be a good friend to you if you let him. We both will.'

Mrs Smee's voice was faltering. Claudia opened her eyes queasily. 'I'm going to miss him so much,' Mrs Smee was whispering, tears beginning to roll down her cheeks.

Claudia fell asleep after that, and Mrs Smee quietly moved her things into Fern's room. It was breakfast time next day before they met again – by which time they were both so fresh and alert that it was hard for either quite to believe in what they'd seen of the other the previous evening. 'There's just one thing I feel I ought to say,' said Mrs Smee as they finished their toast. She tilted her head and ran her eyes over the ceiling before bringing them level with Claudia's. 'All that silly drinking has got to stop, hasn't it?'

'I'm sorry you had to clean up that awful mess.'

'Your aunt had a problem with drink, didn't she? It can go in families, that sort of thing – a sort of weakness.'

'Drink wasn't Belle's problem,' muttered Claudia. 'It was a solution to her problems. If you want to see alcoholics, look out of the window, not at my aunt. She wasn't weak, and weakness does not run in our family.'

Picture postcards arrived from Fern and Wilf. They'd spent a couple of nights at Tod's, they said. The house was getting very damp. Plans would have to be made for it. Idly it crossed Claudia's mind that they ought to have asked her permission before trespassing on her property. But mainly she was glad they'd been. She'd never go back herself. It wasn't her fault she didn't like the place. Belle had got it all wrong. She wasn't a Spark – she'd spent fourteen years telling everyone that. She wasn't interested in preserving the family home. It had been a shock when Belle had died, but she hadn't been essential after all. Everyone was still standing. An old woman and her dreams had simply passed on. Life was like that.

14

Fern and Wilf returned from their honeymoon to find the house in good order and Claudia and Mrs Smee at ease. Their relief at finding that their absence had caused no hardship for anyone else made them more than usually lovey-dovey as they sat down to talk about where they'd been. Fern's fingers wove in and out of Wilf's. She turned to gaze at him whenever Claudia or Mrs Smee were speaking, as if willing to sacrifice their remarks for another sight of him. Wilf, fatigued from the drive, leaned sleepily back on the sofa, his eyes hazy for once. When they went upstairs to unpack Mrs Smee whispered to Claudia. 'They've had a wonderful time. I'm so glad we could look after each other and let them go.'

'It's all right for you,' grumbled Claudia. 'When you've gone I'll be a big gooseberry.'

'Stop feeling so sorry for yourself. Everybody's very proud of you and wants you very much. You've been perfectly all right for the whole week. Don't be difficult now, just because you can see they're happy.'

Claudia picked up some homework and wandered upstairs. ' 'Bye, Mrs Smee,' she called from the landing. 'Thanks for babysitting.'

'I'm afraid I put my foot in it with Claudia, at the very last minute,' Mrs Smee confessed to Wilf on the way to the station. 'She's very jealous of you and Fern. I'm afraid I was cross.' Wilf bought her a ticket and found her a comfortable seat on the train. 'Good luck!' she mouthed at him through the glass. She wished he'd go. He was obviously dying to get back to his new family. She wished that, like Claudia, she had a perfect right to be staying on too . . .

Claudia had left her bedroom door open. She watched through slit eyes as Fern and Wilf crept past to their bedroom. She heard the floor creaking and some soft bumps and laughter. Wilf hurried past her door on his way to the bathroom. His pyjamas were pale blue. She heard the flush of the lavatory. From now on, he'd be using it all the time – perhaps trying the door handle while she was in there . . . After Wilf, Fern scuttled along. On her way back she leaned into Claudia's room. 'Cloddie, you asleep?' Claudia didn't reply. Fern closed the door quietly and switched off the landing light. Claudia's eyes stared into the darkness. Any minute now they'd be starting up. She ought to have let them see she was awake. They wouldn't have done anything then.

End-of-term tests came early to give the staff time to mark and allocate classes for the following year. As the lists went up, it became clear that Claudia was now, to all intents and purposes, top of the class. Anna had beaten her in Art. Others had won awards for games and gymnastics, but that was all. On her way home one evening, she was waylaid by three boys from her year who emptied her school-bag in the gutter, splashed paraffin over her books, and set fire to them, threatening reprisals if they were reported. Claudia did report them and the headmaster made an example of them, caning all three. Results like Claudia's were what he wanted to see, he said. Bullies beware! Few children sided with Claudia, however. It was felt there were other ways in which she could have settled the score. Pupils generally began to shun her as a goody-goody and a sneak, and those attempting to defend her, notably Anna and Sylvie, ran the risk of a tarring with the same brush.

Anna's defence of Claudia was half-hearted. For one thing, she couldn't have said for sure if she still considered herself Claudia's friend or not. At the wedding, Claudia had seemed to take offence every time she opened her mouth. In any case, the invitation had come out of the blue and not been followed up. Second, and more important, her own exam results were causing her mother such anguish that self-defence was taking up most of her resources. Mrs Hackman had lost the battle with her nerves. Her grief for Belle had turned to rage. Belle had been a drunken menace. Mrs Lamont had said as much. She'd taken the Hackmans in with all her cosy talk and then died off, leaving them to pick up the pieces. Mrs Hackman bitterly regretted ever having sold her old piano to make way for Belle's, the sight and sound of which were now a daily affront. Thanks to Belle's advice, Anna had ended up practically bottom of the class.

But it was Mr Hackman's attitude to their problems which eventually tipped his wife right off balance. One night, Mrs Hackman invaded her husband's marking room and announced that the only way to proceed was to remove Ralph from his boarding-school so that the fees could be split to afford private schooling, at day schools, for both their children. Mr Hackman pulled at his moustache for fully a minute before striking his thigh with his hand and pronouncing her suggestion monstrous. Ralph was a bright boy, he said. He'd earned the place at his school and was doing well there. Anna, on the other hand, might or might not be clever – on present showing it seemed unlikely. All the money in the world could never change that, and, in any case, to his way of thinking, a girl's education was a relatively minor matter. If she was passably pretty – as Anna certainly was – it could safely be assumed that some man would eventually take her on.

Mrs Hackman made no attempt to argue. She left the room without demur, as if for an early night. By the next morning, as two years previously, almost to the day, she had become utterly withdrawn, refusing to be coaxed into speech or movement of any kind. After a couple of days, Dr Sylvester advised a return to the hospital. It was a recurrence of the old problem, he said. But she wasn't beyond recall. They shouldn't lose hope.

'I feel like one of those spacemen floating around in a capsule,' Anna told Sylvie. 'There's nothing to pin me down. I don't know what to do with myself. Half the time I'm turning somersaults and thinking it's fantastic, and the other half I'm just dizzy and sick.'

Mr Hackman took care of her as best he could. 'I don't think I'm much use with girls,' he confessed the day after the ambulance took his wife away. 'We always said I'd bring up any boys we had and Cynthia could handle the girls. I didn't expect this.'

'I'm not so different from Ralph, Dad,' said Anna. 'I don't need special treatment.'

Mr Hackman shook his head and sent her off to play the piano. He worked out a list of meal times and a rota for shopping. They must be economical, he said – they both had a cooked meal at school, so they could manage on snacks the rest of the time. To his relief, Sylvie began inviting Anna home after school for tea, and to do their homework together. Mrs Lamont rang up to establish this on a regular footing. In the end, Mr Hackman was able to shut himself away with his marking and his writing for longer than ever.

'I think we should ask Claudia to come home with us, one day,' said Sylvie. 'I think she was trying to make friends again, asking us to the wedding. The next move should come from us.' They were sitting in the basement, their homework spread over a Formica-topped table. In the garden, Raymond and Jack were playing cricket. They did their homework later than the girls, taking over the same table when Sylvie and Anna went upstairs for music practice.

'What about Ray?' said Anna. 'I thought you didn't want Claudia around for his sake.'

'He must be over that by now. It was ages ago. I think we should invite her. I'm quite curious to hear how she's getting on with Wilf, aren't you?'

'Ask her at school if that's all you want to know.'

'It'd be nice to get back to how we used to be. She could be quite a laugh when she was in a good mood. It's boring without her, don't you think so?'

'Thanks,' said Anna, bending low over her diagram of a kidney. 'She practically drove my mother into the loony bin, you know. If she hadn't decided to come top in almost every subject there is . . .'

'Don't be an idiot. She came top because she's clever. She didn't decide anything.'

'She did it to get at me. You haven't known her as long as I have. I know how she works. If she'd been any pal of mine she'd've let me come top in something.'

'Let's face it,' murmured Sylvie. 'You wouldn't have come top whatever she'd done. You were miles down the lists.'

'She wasn't to know that,' said Anna, looking up crossly and brushing the hair out of her eyes. 'All she wanted was to beat me herself. I know exactly what she was doing. It's been like that for ages. If you want her here, ask her instead of me.'

'You'll have to come. It's all arranged with your dad.'

Claudia was greatly surprised by the invitation to East Edge. Sylvie and Anna seemed to have become inseparable since Mrs Hackman's relapse. Claudia had heard that they had taken her side following the caning of the three boys but they hadn't sought her company. She didn't care. There was no common ground between them any more. Polite chit-chat was all their conversation would amount to. They didn't know her now, and she no longer wanted to know them or involve herself in their trivial preoccupations. She assumed they'd stuck up for her for old times' sake, or because they'd genuinely believed in her stand.

At home, she spent hours in her bedroom, working or playing her flute – trying to avoid the sight of Fern and Wilf together. Their affection for one another stifled her. They seemed always to be in contact, either literally or through looks and quick whispers. She escaped upstairs, gasping for air. Only when one of them was out would she come down and engage the other in surprisingly mature conversation. Fern and Wilf were under the impression that she had adapted very smoothly to the changes in the house. They were delighted with her examination results and took her out for a Chinese meal on the strength of them, considering it a lucky break that her passion for study had coincided with their marriage. They spent most evenings in each other's arms on the sitting-room sofa. They had no idea that at night Claudia squeezed wax plugs into her ears till they hurt.

Raymond was the first to see Claudia as she pedalled down the quiet side road towards East Edge. His heart banged and he was glad his blush would have come and gone before Jack could connect it with her appearance.

'Here comes your old heart-throb,' muttered Jack a minute later. 'Let's ignore her.'

Claudia freewheeled through the gate and leaned her bike against the wall. Jack and Raymond were knocking stumps into the ground. She called 'Hello', but they didn't hear. Sylvie saw her from the basement and opened the glass door. 'Hi,' she said. Anna was sitting tensely on a big brown floor cushion. After the sunlight outside, the basement was dark and chill.

'What are you two doing inside?' said Claudia.

'Waiting for you,' said Anna. 'You wouldn't have known where else to look for us, would you?'

Claudia sat down in an old armchair and flicked over the cover of a magazine. 'How's your mother, Anna?'

'Completely mad. You must have heard.'

'Oh, she's not as bad as that,' said Sylvie.

'It was the exams that did it. She couldn't face me being a dunce.'

'Nobody would crack up over that,' said Claudia. 'It isn't your fault.'

'I didn't come top, that's all.'

'You should tell your mother that, if you had, you'd've ended up being mugged in the street. That would cheer her up.'

They joined the boys in the garden. Mrs Lamont, pausing in an upstairs window, thought again how right it had been to move away from London. The twins, especially Raymond, would have been clumsy and gauche there, confined to carpeted rooms, picking their way round fine furniture. As she watched, Claudia sent a ball flying over the top of Jack's head. He sprinted after it. 'A six! A six!' shrieked pretty little Anna whose mother had lost her senses, and Claudia, whose mother had just found hers, streaked back and forth between the stumps. Mrs Lamont's eyes rested fondly on Sylvie. She'd stretched herself out in the sun, her skirt pulled up above her knees. What tormented little souls she'd picked as friends!

The most Raymond could hope for was that nobody would realize how deeply he adored Claudia. He couldn't help himself! He didn't care how many runs she scored – the more the better, so that he could watch her smooth, strong legs dashing back and forth over the grass. The sun was hot and the air heavy with the smell of grass-cuttings. Small birds darted silently in and out of the shrubbery. He flung himself down on the grass beside Sylvie and let out a deep sigh.

'You're keeping your cool, I hope,' she murmured, turning over to look at him.

They had tea together in the basement – bread and peanut butter or marmite. Mrs Lamont opened the door at the top of the stairs and called down that she'd made a chocolate cake. 'He's gone off you, Cloddie,' Sylvie whispered as Raymond went off to fetch it. 'You can relax.'

'I didn't mind him being on me,' said Claudia. 'I don't know why everyone jumped to that conclusion.'

'I've got something for later,' whispered Sylvie. 'Just for the three of us.'

The something was a half-bottle of vintage wine sneaked from her father's wine-rack. When they were on their own, she pulled it from under the old sofa and held it up by the neck. 'Look! It's really good! I thought we'd drink to Tod's and the memory of Aunt Belle. She'd be glad we're together again. She wouldn't have wanted us to drift apart. Let's decide to be friends again – now – properly – before the end of term. Then we can muck around together in the holidays.' She fetched cups and uncorked the bottle, refusing to pour till Claudia and Anna had agreed.

A week or so later, after the schools had broken up, Raymond's letter arrived at Number Nine. Claudia read it at breakfast and returned it to its envelope without comment.

'Anything interesting?' asked Wilf.

'From one of Sylvie's brothers. A real drip.'

Wilf smiled ruefully. 'Poor chap! You'd better tell him not to waste his time.'

'I don't care what he does with his time,' said Claudia. 'But he's not wasting any of mine.'

Later she showed the letter to Anna and Ralph. She had taken to creeping past the window of Mr Hackman's room and down the side of the house to the kitchen door. The visits made Anna tense. She sat on the front of her chair, expecting Claudia's eyes and tone to harden at any moment. 'What makes her think we want to see her?' said Ralph. 'What gives her the right to walk straight in, without even knocking?'

'I don't know,' Anna said. 'I can't think why she comes. We weren't very friendly at all last term – till Sylvie forced us to patch it up.'

Anna and Ralph were still eating their breakfast as Claudia came in. They were subdued, dreading a visit to the hospital in the afternoon. 'You might knock,' said Ralph edgily. 'You've no right to barge in.'

Claudia slid into a chair in the corner. 'I didn't want your dad knowing I was here. I'm not his absolutely favourite guest.' She took a mug of coffee from Anna and crouched over it. 'Hope you're not still blaming me, Anna. I won't be top next year anyway. I've had enough of it.'

'You can't give up now, Cloddie! Not now you're in all the A bands!'

'Blaming you for what?' said Ralph.

Anna went red. 'Cloddie came top in almost everything. But it wouldn't have mattered who it was. It was the fact that I didn't that finished Mum.'

'Don't be idiotic,' said Ralph. 'Nobody'd go nuts over that.'

'That's what I said,' said Claudia. 'Mind you, I don't suppose it helped. She's always tried to pretend they were giving Anna as good a chance as you and it just about proved they weren't. That's how she saw it, I expect. Quite right! Just in terms of money, it's never been fair. How can you spend a fortune on one child and nothing on the other and call it fair? It doesn't really matter which kind of school is better. Purely financially, they've been favouring you. It'd drive anyone mad trying to see it any other way.'

Ralph had been stirring a spoon round and round his mug. He jumped to his feet and stormed over to Claudia's chair, his face changing from white to crimson. 'Now you've bloody finished giving us your analysis of the situation, you can get out!'

Claudia sat back unperturbed. 'Rage away, Ralphie boy,' she said. 'What do *you* think has driven your mother round the bend? Maybe she doesn't get along with your dad as well as she should.'

Ralph was returning to his seat. His face was ashen again. 'Shut your face. What about your own parents, anyway? I should think you must be cramping their style completely.'

Claudia ignored him. She was pulling something from her pocket and handing it to Anna. 'That idiot Raymond has started up again.'

Anna took the letter and read it aloud. 'Sylvie seems to have stirred him up again, doesn't she?' she said afterwards. 'It sounds as if she's told him you fancy him after all.'

'I know how she got that impression. It was that time at their house – d'you remember? She said he'd gone off me, so I thought it was safe enough to say something reasonably pleasant. I didn't mean it.'

'Oh, dear,' said Anna. 'How're you going to wriggle out of it? Sylvie'll get all steamed up again.'

Ralph stood up. 'Someone should just tell him,' he said. 'Deprive you of the chance to make mincemeat of him. Poor bugger.'

More letters arrived and went unanswered. Then, one evening when Wilf and Fern were out, there was a knock on the door of Number Nine and Jack Lamont was standing on the doorstep. He was passing, he said. Would Claudia like to go for a bike ride? The hot day had ended in a cool, clear evening. They made their way along side roads to the canal bank and set off along the bumpy towpath. After a mile or two, Jack jumped off his bike suddenly and leaned it against a tree. Dusk was settling over the water. Twenty yards to their left a lighted holiday barge was moored close to the bank. Through its open door came the clear sound of voices and the clink of pans. 'Come and sit down,' whispered Jack. 'They won't see us.' Claudia sat down beside him. He was about to start pleading for Raymond, she thought. She had no idea what she was going to say . . .

That night Claudia undressed and stood in front of her mirror. Jack hadn't wanted to talk about Raymond at all. He had wanted to kiss her and slip his hands under her clothes. 'We're not kids any more,' he'd whispered. 'Our parents are scared of us really – and jealous. That's why they try to keep us down.'

'I know. Mum would have a fit if she could see me. She's a bloody hypocrite. You should see her and Wilf.' Claudia had been astonished and excited. For a time she'd continued to think that

Jack was really only there on his brother's behalf, and would soon start putting his case. But when he had made no mention of Raymond, neither had she.

At home, Fern and Wilf had been sitting on the sofa together with their feet up. 'Hi,' Fern had called, hearing the door, but Claudia had gone straight upstairs. Aunt Belle had approved of them. They were the real thing. She gazed at herself in the mirror. 'There's only one you,' Belle had said that night, the last time she had said anything very much. 'One body and soul. Think carefully about what you want to do with yourself.' She'd spoken about David Tattersall then. She'd made a tomb of herself after he'd died, she said, locking him up inside, never mentioning his name, never looking for anyone else. It had been a mistake. David might have had some sort of life in other people's imaginations if she'd talked about him. She herself had only half lived. 'Learn from our mistakes,' she'd whispered. 'Fern's and mine. At least Fern is making good before it's too late. Don't ever settle for less than your own Wilf Smee, Cloddie.'

There were no more letters from Raymond. For a time, Claudia confidently awaited another visit from Jack, but he didn't come either. Instead, Sylvie arrived early one morning and hauled Claudia outside on to the pavement to tell her she was a slut and a pig and could keep away from East Edge.

'. . . Perhaps it was because of what you did with Jack,' Anna suggested tremulously. The sight of Claudia quivering on the doorstep alarmed her. It was her first visit for several days. 'Don't speak to her when she does come,' Sylvie had warned. 'She's turning out just like her mother.' But Anna opened the door wider and let Claudia inside.

'How do you know about that? I like Jack. You'd think she'd be pleased. She made enough fuss about me not being crazy about Ray. Jack's really keen on me. I don't know why Sylvie's so mad.'

'It's because Ray's gone into another decline over you. None of them knew he was writing those letters, then Jack walked in the other night and started crowing about you being a push-over. He said he'd taken you down the towpath . . . Oh, Cloddie . . . What happened? . . . He told them you were all over him. He's so vain, he thinks he can get anyone. Don't have anything to do with him. They're off on holiday this week, anyway. They'll be away ages. I don't understand how Jack could be so horrible. He's always been nice to me.'

'Everyone is. – There's no one at home, Anna. Can I stay for a bit?'

'I'd really like you to. Honestly. But Dad and Ralph have to fetch Mum back. She's coming out for a bit. They'll be here any minute. I'm supposed to be tidying up. You know how she always thinks you're a bad influence. . . . And, Cloddie, I'll have to tell you – it was Ralph's fault too.'

'Ralph?'

'When you and Jack were down the towpath that night, Ralph was round at East Edge. He told Ray about you showing us his letter, and what you'd said. He'd never set eyes on Ray before but Sylvie said he just charged into the basement and came out with it. He hates you, Cloddie.'

15

The days became sticky and still. Fern worked longer hours with the American family, whose children were also on holiday from school. Sometimes she brought the children back to Candlemaker Row but they soon became bored without their own things and asked to go home again. 'Come with us, Cloddie,' said Fern. 'Don't hang about here on your own. What do you do all day?'

Even after she'd spoken to Anna, Claudia waited for some sign from Jack, but there was none. The only letter was a bitter parting-shot from Raymond, telling her to ignore his earlier declarations as his opinion of her had altered radically. They were in Scotland, he said. Jack had a girl-friend who spoke Gaelic and did Scottish country dancing in a white dress and tartan sash.

Mrs Hackman did not return to the hospital. The visit home was a success. Anna, in a quick phone call, told Claudia that her mother was even managing to remain calm during extended wrangles with Mr Hackman over the children's education. Neither she nor Ralph had any idea where they'd be ending up next term. Meanwhile, an aunt in Lymington had offered them her house while she was away. It would be their first family holiday for years.

Most days Claudia got up late and flopped on the sofa, eating bowls of cereal in front of the television. It became easy, in the absence of company or homework, to doze until Fern and Wilf came home in the evening. Then, to spare herself the sight of their delight in one another, she put on her green ra-ra skirt and some gold shoes and went down to the Youth Club. 'Where's your posh pals, then?' said Jayne Hooley. 'I thought you were part of the East Edge set.'

Claudia shook her head. 'I'm not allowed near the place.'

'Join the club.' Jayne introduced Claudia to a gang from Ratfield Boys'. Jack Lamont was a bastard, they said. He had it coming to him. It was all planned.

'You can tell me,' said Claudia. 'I'm not in with them now. I never liked them much.'

'Liar!' said Jayne. 'You went down the towpath with Jack. Everyone knows.'

It was a clammy Friday evening. Fern had opened all the windows but the air was motionless. She stopped Claudia on her way out. 'Jayne'll be waiting,' said Claudia. 'What do you want?'

'We've got something to tell you.'

'What is it?'

Wilf stood up and took Fern's hand. 'I'm going to have a baby,' said Fern. 'Not for ages yet, but I wanted you to know straight away. No secrets.'

The plan that Jayne and her friends had revealed to Claudia had struck her as a cross between a very funny and a very sick joke. At best it could be daring and hilarious and at worst . . .

In the end, she managed not to think about the worst very much. It joined the other 'worsts' she was pushing to the back of her mind – Belle's death; Jack's lies; the fact that Sylvie hated her and would be doing her best, after the holidays, to influence Anna; the sickly-sweet devotion between Fern and Wilf; and now this baby, ticking away non-stop like a time bomb, though you couldn't see or hear a thing. 'Don't leave me out,' she said to Jayne. 'Tell me when it's happening. I could do with a good laugh.'

They met outside the Red Lion at ten o'clock in the evening, mostly boys with cans of beer and cigarettes, some on foot and some on bicycles. It was going to be a really good do, they snorted. Really great! Cars and lorries rushed by as they cavorted along the rough verges in the dusk. Once a boy on a bicycle lurched out into the road. Horns blared and an angry face hung from the window of a high cab. As they turned down the dark lane to East Edge, they grew silent. Jayne Hooley squeezed up to Claudia. 'Have a fag,' she whispered. 'I've got a pack of twenty no one knows about.' Claudia shook her head but Jayne stuck two in the corner of her mouth, lit them with the same match and passed one over.

'This is going to be fantastic!' she sniggered. 'I've been dying for this.'

At the bottom of the hill, East Edge was sunk in shadows. The group thinned out and those at the front switched on bicycle lamps and slipped through the gates. As they spotted the basement steps, they flung their bikes down and broke into a shambling run.

The sound of shattering glass seemed to ring in Claudia's ears for minutes on end. She clutched Jayne. 'What did they do that for?' By the time, last in line, she picked her way gingerly through the jagged hole in the glass door, her insides were churning. She crouched in a corner as lamps flashed and people tore open cupboards. Five or six thundered up the wooden stairs into the main body of the house. Those left in the basement giggled in the dark.

Suddenly, as someone found the mains, lights went on everywhere. Jayne jumped to her feet. She rifled through Jack's record collection and turned the player up to full blast. Two boys appeared at the top of the stairs dragging a wine rack. One of them had acquired a heavy spanner with which he was cleanly slicing the tops off the bottles. 'Let's stay down here,' said Claudia as the others swarmed up the stairs. 'Let's get a bottle and have it down here.' They stayed on, dancing together, till the record came to an end. It was only when it stopped that they were suddenly aware of what was going on upstairs. 'They're pulling the place apart,' whispered Jayne. 'Let's clear off. They've gone mad.' She grabbed Claudia by the sleeve and pulled her towards the door.

At the top of the steps they stopped dead, caught like rabbits in the headlights of a car sweeping in through the gates. They huddled together, making no attempt to escape, as two policemen raced past them and a third seized their elbows and propelled them back the way they had come.

Wilf came for Claudia. He stood in the doorway, tense and beaky-nosed. 'Your daughter, sir?'

Wilf nodded.

'He's married to my mother, that's all.'

In the car, Wilf said, 'I'm glad Fern's away. She can be spared all this.'

'Not if they press charges. That's what the policemen told Jayne and me. If the Lamonts press charges we'll end up in court.'

'They won't press charges,' said Wilf.

Later he stood over her bed, looking down at her. How skinny and small she was – still, in many ways, a little girl, with her bony shoulders and the smooth soles to her upturned bare feet. And her sobs were childlike. 'Oh, come on, Cloddie. I didn't think you ever cried.'

'I've got plenty to cry about, haven't I?'

'Tell me what,' said Wilf. He sat down on the floor, leaning against the edge of Claudia's bed so that she was staring at the wiry back of his head. 'What exactly have you got to cry about?'

'You know bloody well,' muttered Claudia. 'Why do you want me to spell it out? Not that I care. I'm past caring.' Wilf's head nodded. 'You've pushed me out. You've taken Mum and made a different family with her. Soon she'll be someone else's mother. You've pushed me out, Wilf bloody Smee. You've managed it.'

Wilf spun round and seized Claudia so tightly round the wrist that for an instant she thought he was going to attack her. 'Oh, Cloddie,' he whispered. 'We've messed you up, haven't we?' He let go of her wrist and went out, closing the door behind him. She heard his feet on the stairs and sprang to the door, opening it a crack to listen.

Claudia lost count of how long she squatted by the door. What was he doing? Had he finished with her? Was he phoning Fern at the Open University course to tell her to come home? At last she tiptoed stiffly downstairs. Wilf was sitting by the gas fire, staring at the curtains, a glass of whisky beside him.

'You look like Aunt Belle,' whispered Claudia. 'With your booze.'

'Do I? Don't hang about in the hall, Cloddie. I want to talk to you.'

She made herself a mug of cocoa and sat on the rug by the fire.

'Let's go to Tod's tomorrow,' said Wilf.

'What about the library?'

'What about it? I think we should go. It's time we made a few decisions.'

'I've decided. I want to sell up. I'd be rich then, wouldn't I?'

'On one way, I suppose you would. And poor in other ways.'

'What ways?'

'Let's go tomorrow,' said Wilf, 'and see.'

Claudia sat in the front of the car, in Fern's seat. Wilf opened the windows and turned on the car radio. 'Let's get in the holiday mood,' he said.

'What about yesterday?' said Claudia. 'What if the Lamonts make a fuss?'

'They won't. There's time to get the place cleaned up before they come home. And I'll speak to Dr Lamont myself.'

'What can you say?'

'It'll depend what he says. But it'll be all right.'

Tod's was a forlorn sight, unkempt and shabby in the sunshine amidst the rich green of its surroundings. The hedge had sprouted bushy and thick, and grass had grown in clumps along the bottom of the gate, making it impossible to open. Wilf had brought the back-door key. 'Run and open the door, Cloddie, while I get our things out of the boot.'

Claudia climbed the gate and ran over the weedy pebbles to the back door. It was a tricky lock – Aunt Belle had often stood shaking at it, vowing to have it fixed. Claudia stood now, fiddling and straining, hearing Belle's voice. 'Damn thing! Playing the fool! It only does it on wet days.' But today the sun was shining. Suddenly and easily, when Claudia least expected it, the key slipped round and the door opened. A shaft of sunlight fell across the floor and the kitchen table. Claudia poked her head round the door. Belle's chair was still there, with a pair of her slippers tucked underneath. Claudia went in. She reached out to the Aga but it was cold. 'I never let the Aga out,' Belle's voice said. 'It's like a heart pumping away. I keep it in all summer. It's always chilly on this side of the house.' Claudia ran to the door. Wilf heard her thin voice calling, 'Wilf, we must light the Aga.'

In the sitting-room, the family photographs were thick with dust. There was a patch on the carpet where the piano had been.

The Hackmans had snatched it away weeks ago, before there could be any argument. The room looked strange without it. A portrait of Great Grandma Spark, done in oils by a family friend, gazed discontentedly down from the fireplace. 'She was a jolly woman,' said Belle. 'Nothing like that at all. She thought the painting was a hoot.' Claudia crossed the hall, stepping over the rag rugs that Granny Spark had made, crouching on her knees for hours at a time. At the top of the stairs, the bathroom door was ajar. A toothbrush of Belle's dangled from its holder above the taps. A bottle of lavender-water stood on the window-ledge. Claudia darted past. At the end of the passage was her own bedroom – the one she'd shared with Anna and Sylvie.

It had been left almost untouched since their last visit. On the dressing-table sat a worn teddy-bear of Belle's which she'd long ago passed on to Claudia. Outside the window, the leaves of the pear tree were absolutely still. The camp beds used by Anna and Sylvie were folded against the wall. Beside them was a neat pile of oddments they'd left behind – an exercise book of Anna's, three hair clips, an empty purse and a red sock. Claudia sat on the bed. She could smell the sandalwood perfume Sylvie had brought the last time. She'd dropped the bottle on the carpet and they'd spent hours scrubbing at it with face flannels and sponges. Every time they'd washed afterwards they'd ended up smelling of the stuff. It was a long time before Claudia's eye lit on a card propped up on the mantelpiece. It was a photograph of herself as a baby, in her pram under the pear tree. It had been mounted on a piece of white card and underneath Belle had written: 'Welcome Home.' Claudia examined it in astonishment. Had it stood there, unnoticed, all through their last visit? Or had Belle put it there some time later?

When Claudia came down, Wilf was sitting in Belle's chair reading the paper. 'I've done my best with this thing,' he said, poking his foot at the Aga. 'We'll have to see what happens.'

Claudia sat down at the table. 'Could you imagine ever living here, Wilf?'

'That's what we'll have to decide, isn't it?'

Claudia nodded and held out the photograph she'd found upstairs. 'I don't know when Belle left this.'

Wilf took the card. 'Mmm. I wouldn't take too much notice, Cloddie. Emotional blackmail, if you ask me.'

'I don't think she really meant it that way. I think she thought I wanted to live here. I think I gave her that impression.'

'But you don't.'

Claudia took back the card and propped it against the salt pot. 'I don't really know. I do like the place. It does feel a bit like coming home. And I can't imagine just anyone living here. Do you know, I can actually remember that photograph being taken? Mum was tipping right over – to get the right angle, I suppose. She was wearing a red skirt.'

'If we do sell it – if that can be sorted out legally – we shan't get much of a price for it, you know. It's pretty run down.'

'The odd thing is how different it seems now Belle's gone. I thought it'd be drearier than ever, but it isn't. It must have been her that made the whole place gloomy. That sounds awful. It isn't that I didn't love her, but it's just such a relief to be finished with all that sadness and loneliness and illness. Anna and Sylvie never really saw that side of her – in fact things were a lot better once they started coming here – they weren't so wrapped up in the family side of it. I'll never forget sitting up with Belle the last night. She made me feel as if one day I'd have to take her place. I had visions of myself fifty years on, just like her.'

'It's a pity she put you through that.'

'It wasn't her fault, Wilf. I kept asking her things. I wanted her to talk that way, really, but when she did, it was too much. She kept on saying I was a Spark and this was a Spark house and never the two should part and all that sort of thing.'

'And, of course, we know you're nothing of the kind! You've told us often enough.'

Claudia smiled. 'Funny thing is that here we are – you definitely not a Spark at all, and me half a Spark and pretending not to be – and, for once, I get an inkling of what Belle was on about. You can tell there's only ever been one family living here, can't you? You can tell it hasn't gone through loads of upheavals changing hands all the time. There *is* a family feel to it, isn't there?'

'I'm sure you're right,' said Wilf. 'I certainly feel very comfortable here – not that it's my family, of course. The thing is, is it yours? Do you get that feeling after all?'

'Just a bit. Now Belle's not nagging about "roots" and "ancestors". When I was little I loved coming. It was only when I had to come on my own I started not liking it. Belle was old and lame and I guessed she wasn't happy, though she never took it out on me. I didn't know what was the matter with her really – I wasn't that bothered. I was fed up with Mum for packing me off. I didn't see why we had to have so much to do with Belle. I didn't care if she was our only living relative. Then, when Anna and Sylvie thought she was great, I got jealous. I started thinking she liked Anna best. She seemed to be so worried about her all the time. And I always resented the fact that she never took my dad into account. She never mentioned him.'

Wilf leaned forward suddenly. 'Let's get one thing straight, Cloddie. You're as much of a Spark as any of the people who ever lived here. Even Aunt Belle was only half a Spark, as you put it. Her mother was a something else. I'm only half a Smee, come to that. My mother was a Johnson. What it boils down to is, do you want to live in this house? Its previous owners have been relatives of yours, which might give it an added appeal over other bricks and mortar – on the other hand, you might prefer to shake their dust off your feet. Whatever happens, you'll be living with Fern and me and the baby. We're all trailing ancestors, whether we're aware of them or not, but what really shapes our lives is our living family. Is that right?' The sun was shining in Claudia's eyes. She blinked, trying to see through it. 'Belle left a letter for Fern, you know . . . She was very concerned that you shouldn't feel muddled about where you fit in – specially with Fern and me about to marry. She thought leaving you the house would steady you up. Fern wasn't sure that uprooting you from school and friends was the right thing to do. You didn't seem to want to come. So we shelved the whole idea. We didn't want to hurt you, Cloddie.'

The sun was like a spotlight. From behind it, Wilf was searching her mind with his pin-point eyes. 'Fern's hurt me from the moment I was born,' muttered Claudia. 'You were the last straw.' She leaned down low over the old table. The smell of its scrubbed wooden top filled her head. She and Aunt Belle had drawn pictures here and puzzled over jigsaws and baked sponges and flapjacks. 'I wish Belle wasn't dead. I wasn't very nice to her.'

She was aware of Wilf moving towards her. His arms were round her shoulders and his face was close to hers. 'Cloddie, I want you to know something . . . I wouldn't have married Fern if I hadn't been quite sure that I loved everything about her.' She could smell him now, soapy, immaculate Wilf, rubbing his crinkly head against hers. '. . . Absolutely everything.'

She looked up, feeling in her pocket for a hanky. 'I assumed you did love everything about her. There wouldn't be any point otherwise.'

'Well, you're part of the everything.'

Claudia blew her nose. Sudden giggles caught in her throat. 'Are you trying to tell me you love me too, Wilf?' she snorted. 'Is that it?'

'We've decided to live at Tod's,' Wilf told Fern on the phone that night. He winked through the door at Claudia. 'We're here now – at Tod's. We're going to stay a couple of days. We'll be back when you get home. But we've definitely decided.' He talked on but Claudia stopped listening. She'd lit candles in the kitchen and Wilf had opened wine to have with their bacon and eggs. It was six hours since he'd said he loved her.

'She wants to talk to you,' said Wilf.

'What's going on?' said Fern's voice.

'Wilf and I are staying at Tod's for a few days and we've decided it'd be nice to live here all the time. He says you've been thinking about it for ages. He says he can get a job in Cranwick library.'

'It's not as good as the job he's got.'

'He says he might be able to work his way up again. He wants to live here. He says he likes the country. It'll be nice for your baby too, won't it?'

'I want it to be your choice, Cloddie. I don't want anyone talking you into it. I'm not moving unless it's where *you* want to live.'

'It is,' said Claudia.

'Is he looking after you all right?'

'Yes. I'm making our supper.'

'You sound very grown-up all of a sudden . . .'

'Fern sounded quite jealous of me,' said Claudia, sitting back from the table with her glass. 'What would she say if she'd heard you earlier?'

'She'd be pleased,' said Wilf. 'She wouldn't have married me if she hadn't believed I cared for you.'

'You didn't just kid her on that you liked me? It isn't all just a con to keep her happy?'

Wilf ran his hands through his hair and laughed. 'Good God, Cloddie! You've been flirting like a twenty-year-old all evening and now you look like a toddler lost in a supermarket.'

'Just tell me, though – tell me it's nothing to do with her.'

Wilf reached out and took her hand. 'I love you, Cloddie – in an entirely proper and blameless way. I shall be the father of your half-brother or -sister. If you ever care to look on me as some sort of close relative of your own I'll be extremely happy. But Time's definitely on our side. There's no need to rush.'

Claudia left the curtains open that night and lay in bed staring out at the pear tree. It was quivering now, in moonlight, with shiny, black leaves. She thought of Wilf somewhere else in the house. Tomorrow they were going to work in the garden. They were the first ones home, he had said – and he would never forget their homecoming.

16

Claudia returned reluctantly to Ratfield. 'Now I've made my mind up,' she told Wilf before they set off, 'I wish I could just stay here.' They were having coffee in the open doorway of the kitchen. The sun streamed in, and bright tufts of grass glinted round the step. 'I want everything to stay exactly as it is this minute. I don't really want to see Number Nine again – just in case I change my mind.'

As they drew up at the end of Candlemaker Row, they could see Fern at the living-room window. She was pale. 'What's been going on?' she asked before the door had closed behind them. Her hands moved nervously over her stomach. 'Are we really moving? What changed your mind, Cloddie?'

'She's unbelievable,' Claudia told Anna over the phone. 'She comes over all feeble and trembly at the idea of packing up and removal vans and all that. She's making Wilf nervous. She wants to go, you know. More than anyone. If you ask me, she's just putting it all on so I'll never be able to accuse her of forcing me. She's pathetic.'

Anna's voice was low. 'Are you really going, Cloddie? You sound completely different from the last time I saw you. I thought about you all the time in Lymington. I thought we were going to be friends again.'

'We are. It's going to be better than ever. When can you come round?'

Anna looked taller, standing on the doorstep in a new blue dress. She'd brought her violin. 'I've been learning a lovely piece over the summer,' she said. 'I thought you'd want to hear.'

Claudia let her in. 'Are you scared we're going to run out of things to say or something?'

'I think I might be sad,' said Anna. 'I don't want you to move.'

They sat together in the living-room. Outside, Candlemaker Row was grey and leafless. The bench was deserted. 'I don't know why I thought Tod's was more depressing than this,' said Claudia. 'It was only Aunt Belle, casting a blight on the place.' Anna looked reproachful. 'It wasn't her fault. She just made me feel so guilty.'

'She didn't me,' said Anna. 'She made me feel a lot less guilty, as a matter of fact.'

'That's because you weren't family,' said Claudia. 'You were fed up about that, weren't you? But I think it made it easier for you to get on with Belle really well. You hadn't grown up knowing what a miserable life she'd had. Anyway, I'm glad for her sake we're moving to Tod's. It's what she wanted. It would have cheered her up.'

'She always seemed perfectly cheerful to me. It was only you that got all intense about her. – Anyway, won't Fern and Wilf feel a bit odd, with it being your house?'

'We'll all feel odd. Mrs Smee's coming too, you know. That was my idea. The place is so vast – there's loads of room for her. And if Fern and Wilf are going to be all gooey about the baby at least there'll be someone sane for me. Actually, I've come round to Wilf a bit. We went down to Tod's together, just the two of us. I think he really likes me. He said they'd been worried – wanting me to feel loved and everything, not dying of jealousy over the baby.'

'I heard about the baby when we came back from Lymington,' murmured Anna. 'Someone told Mum. I wondered what you'd think. I've been worried about you myself.'

Claudia stood up suddenly and went to the window, pretending to look out. 'I've missed you, Anna. We've messed things up for a whole year practically. I've had no one to talk to. Have you?'

'Not really,' said Anna. There was Sylvie. She was a friend. But not like Claudia. Nobody was. 'I've missed you too. And I'm going to miss you even more.'

'You can come and stay. Just like when Belle was alive.'

'Are you going to ask Sylvie?'

Claudia shook her head. She'd finished with the Lamonts, she said. She would never have started with them if it hadn't been for Anna's illness at the beginning of the year. She'd been in the gang that had ransacked their house. Had Anna heard?

'I won't tell her,' said Anna. 'I won't say you were there.'

'She'll find out. Wilf's going to get it all sorted out. Jack's a pig, you know. People can't stand him.'

'But there's no point Sylvie hating you.'

'I don't care. We were never real friends. Not like you and me. She never had a clue about how I felt about anything. And she's absolutely warped about Ray. Why can't she see how wet he is?'

'Ray's nice, Cloddie. And Sylvie did like you, you know. You probably don't understand her, either – not deep down.'

'She hasn't got a "deep down",' muttered Claudia. 'Don't let's fight about her. She wouldn't want to come to Tod's, anyway. It'll just be us – if your mum'll let you come.'

'Mum and Dad are different. Ralph's starting at Dad's school after September and I'm going to St Winifred's.'

'My God, Anna! You'll have to wear one of those hats. You'll turn into a prissy little cow! How's your dad going to pay for it all? You'll have them *both* in the Royal!'

Anna laughed. She had the feeling that her family was finished with the Royal. They had taken their rows and differences down to Lymington and screamed at each other for three weeks. They'd returned to Winchester Road and carried on the screaming. 'I think we're mentally rather a tough lot or we'd all be mad by now,' she said. 'If sending me to St Winifred's makes Mum feel so much better, I don't mind going. I'll always be friends with you – she knows that. I won't change.'

'Will she let you come to Tod's?'

'Yes,' said Anna. 'That was one of the fights Dad won. He said Mum had always been a jumped-up snob about your mother, and it wouldn't do her any harm to take a leaf out of Fern's book as far as femininity went.'

'God! What did your mum say?'

'She said there'd be some point if he ever looked up from his bloody marking long enough to notice her.'

Fern and Wilf stayed away from the house all the afternoon. When they came back, Anna was playing her violin in the living-room while Claudia made toasted cheese. 'You play beautifully, Anna,' said Fern. 'You put such a lot of feeling into it. Are you going to be a musician when you leave school?'

'I'm going to try,' said Anna. 'Aunt Belle said if you had a real passion in life you shouldn't ever let it go.'

'Yuk,' said Claudia, standing in the doorway with two plates.

'Wise words, Anna,' murmured Wilf.

They sold Number Nine for a fair price to a young couple whose baby was much more obviously on the way than Fern's. 'It's so pretty,' the woman said to Fern. 'You've kept it beautifully. It makes up for the grot outside.'

'The Row will be nice again one day,' said Fern. 'When the Council gets round to it. We've been very happy here. I'll be sad to move.'

'Will you really?' asked Claudia that afternoon while they were emptying drawers upstairs and packing clothes into tea-chests and cartons. 'Would you rather be staying on here?'

'Not taking everything into account,' said Fern. 'It's a bit miserable, though, isn't it, closing down on a whole phase of your life?'

'A rotten phase. Just you and me at each other's throats for years on end.'

'Rubbish! We've had nice times. You were a stunning little baby. People used to rave about your curls and your smile. And Belle used to come two or three times a month at first. She helped me paint the whole house. She came round the shops with me for curtains and things. She had never set up a home of her own, you know – only that little flat she had in Cranwick when she was teaching. Tod's didn't need setting up – it had been set up for years and years already. I'm going to miss having my own little place.'

'But Tod's is ours. Much more than this. God knows how many people have owned this in its time.'

'I don't mind that. I don't mind other people.'

Claudia put down a pile of towels she'd been about to pack and flopped heavily on the bed. 'I don't believe this! You're going to refuse to budge when it comes to it, aren't you? We're never going to end up at Tod's at all. I thought as long as you'd got Wilf, you didn't care where you moved.'

'You thought wrong, then, didn't you? And not for the first

time, if you don't mind my saying so.' Fern took her wedding dress from the wardrobe and folded it in silence.

'It's mad!' said Claudia. 'Am I the only one that wants to go? What about Wilf? I'm sure he doesn't know you're in a heap about leaving here.'

'Oh, forget it,' said Fern. 'Can't I have a moment's nostalgia? We all want to move – specially Wilf. I don't think he's found it all that easy here – having to fit in with our way of doing things. I think he's felt quite an outsider.'

'Maybe he'll feel even worse at Tod's.'

'I don't think so. It's never been home for any of us.' Fern hesitated. 'And I've never had any sort of private involvement there.'

'What on earth's that supposed to mean?'

'Tod's doesn't hold memories of anybody else, that's all.' Claudia had gone bright red. ' "*Involvement*",' said Fern. 'Not affair! What's wrong? You've got a nerve, turning prudish on me now after all I've put up with from you!'

'Don't tell me anything else,' muttered Claudia. She pulled out one of Fern's dressing-table drawers and emptied it on to the bed.

'Oh!' said Fern. 'I'd better go through that lot myself.'

A bundle of letters had fallen clear of the hankies and underwear. 'What's this?' said Claudia. She picked up the bundle and turned it over. On the other side, tied up with the letters, was a photograph of a boy of about twenty. He was trying to flatten down his mass of curly hair with one hand and shooing away the camera with the other.

'I'll have to get rid of that,' mumbled Fern, 'now we're moving.'

'I should think you will!' whispered Claudia. 'I can guess who it is, you know. Are those his letters? What are they doing here? Does Wilf know?' She stared at the photograph but made no attempt to detach it from the letters or to untie the bundle. 'What're you playing at, Mum? Here's Wilf and me trying to form a relationship, more or less for your sake, and then all of a sudden you produce this little lot. What am I supposed to think? This bloke looks just like me. Why didn't you show me before?'

'I don't know,' muttered Fern. 'I did love him, you know.'

'You should have told him about me, then. He might even have married you.'

'It wouldn't have worked. He was just sorry for me. He did a lot to get me through the first few weeks after Mum and Dad died.'

'What about the letters?'

'He went off to France to do a year abroad as part of his course. He wrote a lot at first but in the end it all just faded out. I never told him I was pregnant. By the time he came back to university, I'd left. People started to talk when I got very fat. I just packed up and went to Tod's. Belle was marvellous.'

'He might have wanted to see me – if he'd known.'

'I know. I used to agonize about whether I had the right to keep you all to myself. But he could have tracked me down if he'd wanted to. Someone must have told him what had happened to me, and several people had my address. I heard from a friend, in the end, that he was marrying someone else and going off to the States. He was awfully witty and brainy. I don't think I could have kept up with him, really.'

Claudia stood up and snatched a cardboard carton from the floor. 'Not like dumb, ordinary old Wilf, you mean.'

In her bedroom she sat on the floor, staring into the empty box. All these years that picture had been five or six yards away, stuffed out of sight under Fern's bras and pants! All the time she'd wondered what her dad had been like, he'd been there with a dozen or so letters – all she'd have needed to form a real impression of him. But now it was too late. Now he was just a menace, turning up to cause trouble for Wilf. Fern was a cheat. She should have cleared all that junk out long ago. She was a spoilt cow. Wilf deserved better.

At supper time, Claudia popped her head around Fern's door. Two huge boxes stood ready for the removal men. The bundle of letters had gone. In the kitchen Fern was standing at the stove. 'I've got rid of them. I hadn't exactly forgotten they were there, but I hadn't looked at them for ages, you know. And I can promise you one thing, when I looked at them this afternoon, it was the first time ever that I didn't feel any sort of pang. I knew I was over him really, but I hadn't wanted to test myself.'

'I'm over him too,' scoffed Claudia. 'He looked a bit shifty to me. At least your dreary little bookworm won't leave you holding the baby this time. You can count on that.' She turned, hearing Wilf's key in the lock, and ran into the hall. When he came in, she was leaning against the stairs gazing towards the door. 'I thought it was you,' she said. 'Good!'

'That's a nice welcome,' said Wilf.

It was the middle of the night. 'Don't be scared,' Fern was whispering, stumbling towards her in the dark. 'It's Mum.'

Claudia reached out and turned on her bedside lamp. 'What is it?'

'I can't sleep, Cloddie. I keep thinking about this afternoon. I feel so awful about what happened and what you must be thinking. The last thing I want is for you to be confused.'

'Where's Wilf?'

'Sleeping. He doesn't know I'm here. I do love him, Cloddie.'

'For goodness' sake go back to bed with him, then. I'm perfectly all right.'

'Am I being ridiculous? It's probably my hormones. You get all upside down when you're pregnant. You'll find out. It's just I can't bear you thinking I don't love Wilf or that I think he's second rate. I don't know why I hung on to those letters – except it was in the back of my mind that you might like to see them one day. We did love each other in a way, you see. It was very intense.'

Claudia turned her head into her pillow and snorted. 'Go back to bed, Mum, or I'll wake Wilf and start telling him about the intensity of my conception!' When Fern didn't reply, she looked round. 'I'm *joking*! OK, I believe you. I don't want to talk about it. He's gone.' She pulled Fern's knotted hands apart and kissed one of them. 'I did that to Belle once,' she giggled. 'She looked just like you – eyes popping out of her head!'

On a wet day in early September they left Candlemaker Row for good. Vandals had broken in through the kitchen window of Tod's the week before. Fern and Mrs Smee stood in the hall surveying the dereliction. 'What a mess!' said Fern. 'You'll wonder why we've been praising the place to the skies. You won't want to live in a dump like this.'

'Don't be silly, dear,' said Mrs Smee. 'We can tackle this in no time.'

'They probably did it just for a lark,' said Claudia. 'It probably got a bit out of hand.'

'The voice of experience,' whispered Wilf. 'Take my mother upstairs and find her a nice bedroom.'

Mrs Smee chose the room next to Claudia's. 'I won't bother you, Cloddie,' she said, shaking off her shoes. 'But it won't do any harm for us to close ranks a little bit. We mustn't feel like oddments if it's our home as well as theirs.'

'It's *my* house,' said Claudia. 'You're all guests of mine really. And I specially wanted you.'

'Thank you, dear,' said Mrs Smee. She sat down on the bed and gazed round at her new surroundings. 'Do you know what I think we should do, Cloddie? I think we should go to the crematorium one day – just you and me. I think we should go and see where your aunt's ashes are scattered.'

'There's no plaque or anything. Her name's on a register, that's all.'

'Just the same, I think we should go. I feel a real bond with Belle myself. We never met, but I'm full of gratitude to her. I feel as if I've been allowed to take her place.'

'I suppose you have. I'd never have thought of it like that because you're so different. – OK, I will go. I wouldn't mind seeing where she is. I still half expect her to turn up in the kitchen, you know. She doesn't feel dead.'

'I know,' said Mrs Smee. 'We'll go on the first fine day. We'll lay her to rest.' She walked round the room, inspecting cupboards and drawers. 'It'll be nice for this old house, coming to life again, won't it? Fern's told me all the history. We must try and make it a real family home again, like the old days. – Would you ever think of changing your name, dear? So we could all be the same.'

'I don't think so. It's taken me all my time to accept being a

Spark – I can't imagine changing myself into something else now. Besides, I'm the only Spark left and there've always been Sparks at Tod's. That's what Aunt Belle kept on and on about.'

'If you're a Spark, you'll be one whatever you call yourself,' observed Mrs Smee pleasantly. 'It's not really the name, dear. It's you.'

Also in Puffin Plus

AN OPEN MIND
Susan Sallis

A subtle and compassionate teenage novel in which David, working as a volunteer at a spastic school, gradually comes to terms with his parents' divorce and its effect on his life.

MARTINI-ON-THE-ROCKS
Susan Gregory

Eight short stories about teenage life in a multi-racial urban setting. From battles with teachers, to a young Hindu wedding, to the problems of being with the in-crowd: an extremely absorbing and contemporary collection.

CLOUDY/BRIGHT
John Rowe Townsend

A sensitive and amusing contemporary love story about two young aspiring photographers. The same events are related alternately by Sam and Jenny, often from very different angles!

ARE YOU LISTENING, KAREN?
David Day

Jay Border is sixteen and shy – and hopelessly in love. Desperate for a sympathetic ear, he sets off to have a long chat with Karen, his sister, now dead. A moving account of adolescent insecurities.

EDITH JACKSON
Rosa Guy

The story of a young black orphan, struggling against poverty and prejudice to keep together the remnants of her family. A sequel to *The Friends*.

NO PLACE LIKE
Gene Kemp

Peter Williams has problems – he fails exams, demolishes bathroom walls, and almost burns the house down. And just when he finally seems to be settling down at sixth form college, trouble looms once more . . .